10 Minute Guide to
Quicken® 6

Linda Fl~~~

D0870902

alpha
books

A Division of Prentice Hall Computer Publishing

11711 North College, Carmel, Indiana 46032 USA

To my girls; Jade, Jordan and Ali.

© 1992 by Alpha Books

International Standard Book Number: 1-56761-019-6
Library of Congress Catalog Card Number: 92-82812

95 94 93 92   8 7 6 5 4 3 2 1

Interpretation of the printing code: the rightmost double-digit number is the year of the book's printing; the rightmost single-digit number is the number of the book's printing. For example, a printing code of 92-1 shows that the first printing of the book occurred in 1992.

Publisher: *Marie Butler-Knight*
Managing Editor: *Elizabeth Keaffaber*
Product Development Manager: *Lisa A. Bucki*
Acquisitions Manager: *Stephen R. Poland*
Production Editor: *Linda Hawkins*
Copy Editor: *Audra Gable*
Editorial Assistant: *Hilary J. Adams*
Cover Design: *Dan Armstrong*
Designer: *Michele Laseau*
Indexer: *Jeanne Clark*
Production Team: *Tim Cox, Mark Enochs, Tim Groeling, Tom Loveman, Carrie Roth, Kelli Widdifield*

Special thanks to Hilary J. Adams for ensuring the technical accuracy of this book.

Screen reproductions in this book were created by means of the program Collage Plus from Inner Media, Inc., Hollis, NH.

Printed in the United States of America

Contents

Introduction

Perhaps your spouse or small-business partner has just purchased Quicken for your computer and asks that you start using the program to automate your finances. Until now, all you've heard about Quicken was that it is a program which allows users to manage their home and business finances. A few things are certain:

- You need to learn the program quickly.

- You need to identify and learn only the tasks necessary to accomplish your particular goals.

- You need a clear-cut, plain-English guide to learn about the basic features of the program.

The *10 Minute Guide to Quicken 6* is designed to teach you the operations you need in short, easy-to-understand lessons that can be completed in 10 minutes or less.

What Is the 10 Minute Guide?

The 10 Minute Guide series is a new approach to learning computer programs. Instead of trying to teach you everything about a particular software product, the 10 Minute Guide teaches you only about the most often-used features.

Each 10 Minute Guide contains over 20 short lessons. The 10 Minute Guide teaches you about programs without relying on technical jargon. You'll find only plain English used to explain the procedures in this book.

The following icons help you find your way around the *10 Minute Guide to Quicken 6*:

 Timesaver Tips offer shortcuts and hints for using the program more effectively.

 Plain English icons identify definitions of new terms.

 Panic Button icons appear at places where new users often run into trouble.

Additionally, a table of shortcut keys is included on the book's inside back cover, providing you with a guide to the key combinations which access Quicken options and features quickly and easily.

Throughout the book, specific conventions are used to help you find your way around Quicken as easily as possible:

What you type	The keys you press and the information you type are printed in bold computer type in color.
What you see	The text you see on-screen will appear in computer type.

Menu names   The names of Quicken
                              menus, options, and activi-
                              ties are displayed with the
                              first letter capitalized.

Menu selections   The letters you press to pull
                              down menus and activate
                              menu options are printed in
                              bold type.

The *10 Minute Guide to Quicken 6* is organized in 22
lessons, ranging from basic startup to more advanced file
management features. Remember, however, that nothing in
this book is difficult. Most users want to start at the
beginning of the book with the lesson on starting Quicken
and progress (as time allows) through the lessons sequen-
tially.

Who Should Use the *10 Minute Guide to Quicken 6*?

The *10 Minute Guide to Quicken 6* is for anyone who:

- Needs to learn Quicken quickly.

- Doesn't have a lot of time to spend learning a
  new program.

- Wants to find out quickly whether Quicken will
  meet his or her computer needs.

- Wants a clear, concise guide to the most important features of the Quicken program.

You say your time is important to you and that you need to make the most of it. The *10 Minute Guide to Quicken 6* will help you learn this extremely popular and powerful program in a fraction of the time you might ordinarily spend struggling with new software.

What Is Quicken 6?

Quicken is a home and business finance program that helps keep track of your income and expenses. With Quicken, you can:

- Write and print checks.

- Reconcile your bank account.

- Keep track of your assets, liabilities, and net worth.

- Create monthly budgets.

- Amortize loans.

- Generate detailed reports.

- View on-screen graphs to analyze your finances.

- Plan for the future using Quicken 6's new financial calculators.

Additionally, Quicken automatically reminds you of checks to print with the Billminder feature and enables you to pay bills electronically, although these features are not covered in this 10 Minute Guide.

For Further Reference...

Consult *The First Book of Quicken 6* by Alpha Books.

Trademarks

All terms mentioned in this book that are known to be trademarks or service marks are listed below. In addition, terms suspected of being trademarks or service marks have been appropriately capitalized. Alpha Books cannot attest to the accuracy of this information. Use of a term in this book should not be regarded as affecting the validity of any trademark or service mark.

Quicken is a registered trademark of Intuit.

CheckFree is a trademark of Checkfree Corporation.

Lessons

Lesson 1
Getting Started
with Quicken

In this lesson, you'll learn how to start and end a typical Quicken session. You will also learn how to use the Main menu and various pull-down menus.

Starting Quicken

If you installed Quicken 6 according to the instructions on the inside front cover of this book, follow these steps:

1. Start your system.

2. At the C:> prompt, type q and press Enter.

The Main menu appears as shown in Figure 1.1. (Depending on how you installed Quicken, numbers may appear beside the Main menu choices. The version with the numbers leads to *Function-Key menus*, explained in the next section, "Using Quicken's Menu Access Styles.")

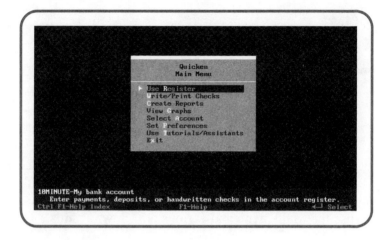

Figure 1.1 The Main menu.

Note: The first time that you start the program, Quicken displays the First Time Setup window to select standard categories and the location for your data files. See Lesson 2 for more on setting up Quicken.

Using Quicken's Menu Access Styles

Quicken activities or options are accessed through the Main menu. Quicken 6 includes two menu access styles: *Function-Key menus* and *Alt-Key menus*. If you are updating from Quicken 1.0, 2.0, 3.0, or 4.0, the default menu access style is the Function-Key menu. If you are installing Quicken for the first time or updating from Quicken 5, the default menu access style is the Alt-Key menu. This lesson explains both menu access styles. For the rest of this book, lessons will be explained using the Alt-Key menu access style. Note that you can change the menu access style by setting a preference in Quicken. Refer to Lesson 2 to learn how to set preferences.

Using Function-Key Menus

You can select program options from a Function-Key menu (such as the one shown in Figure 1.2) using one of the following methods:

- Press the number or letter that corresponds to the activity or option that you want to select. For example, to select the Create Reports option from the Main menu shown in Figure 1.2, press 3.

- Move the cursor using the Up and Down Arrow keys to the option you want to select. Press Enter. For example, to select the Write/Print Checks option, move the cursor to the Write/Print Checks line and press Enter.

- Press a shortcut (Ctrl-key) combination. Shortcut keys are listed on the inside back cover. For example, to select the Use Register option, press Ctrl-R. (Not all Main menu options can be accessed using a shortcut key.)

Press a number to select an option.

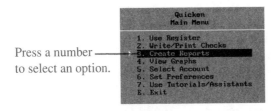

Figure 1.2 The Main menu with the Function-Key menu style.

3

Using Alt-Key Menus

You can select program options from Alt-Key menus (such as the one shown in Figure 1.3) using one of the following methods:

- Press the highlighted letter in the menu or option name. For example, to select Use **R**egister, press R.

- Move the cursor using the Up and Down Arrow keys to the option that you want to select and press Enter. For example, to select the Select **A**ccount option, move the cursor to the Select Account line and press Enter.

Press the highlighted letter, or use the arrow keys plus Enter to select a command.

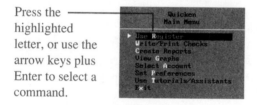

Figure 1.3 The Main menu with the Alt-Key menu style.

Using Pull-Down Menus

After you've selected one of the Main menu options, Quicken displays the opening screen for that activity. Some screens offer pull-down menus to access program options.

Pull-Down Menu A menu that remains hidden within a menu bar until you open or *pull down* the complete menu. The complete menu contains additional options, features, and functions. After you access the pull-down menu, you may select any of the options.

To select an option, feature, or function from a Quicken pull-down menu, press the highlighted letter within the option name or press the Alt key in combination with the highlighted letter within the option name. If you are using a mouse, point and click on the option name.

For example, to select the Void Transaction option from the Register screen, follow these steps:

1. Select the account you want to work with. (Lesson 3 explains how to set up and select accounts. You might even want to create a sample account to try out this pull-down menu selection procedure.)

2. Press Alt-E to pull down the Edit pull-down menu as shown in Figure 1.4.

3. Press V to select the Void Transaction option from the Edit pull-down menu.

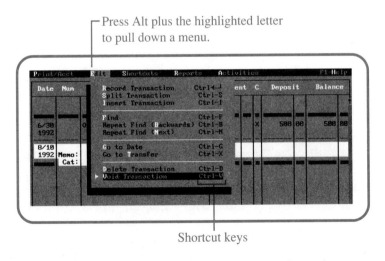

Press Alt plus the highlighted letter
to pull down a menu.

Shortcut keys

Figure 1.4   The pull-down Edit menu from the Register screen.

Using Shortcut Keys Many options in pull-down menus can be selected using shortcut keys. A shortcut key is a combination of the Ctrl key and a letter key pressed simultaneously. There is no need to access the pull-down menu to use shortcut keys. Simply press the shortcut keys from a register screen, the Write Checks screen, a Report screen, or a Budget screen.

Using the Keyboard

Your keyboard can be used to select menu options and commands and to move around Quicken screens.

Throughout the remainder of this book, the term *select*, for keyboard users, will mean one of the following:

- Press the highlighted letter in the menu or option name.

- Move the cursor to the menu or option name and press Enter.

Using a Mouse

Mouse support is available with Quicken. You can use any Microsoft-compatible mouse to select pull-down menus, menu commands and options, move around the screen, display windows, or select items from lists. To perform most Quicken operations with a mouse, simply point and click.

Point and Click To point to an item on the screen, move the mouse pointer to highlight the item on the screen. Then press and release (click) the left mouse button.

This book will explain *keyboard* steps for performing operations in Quicken. Therefore, if you are using a mouse, note the following procedures:

Operation	Mouse Procedure
Choose an item from a list	Double-click.
Scroll up or down a register or a list	Hold down the mouse on a transaction or list item and move the mouse up or down. Hold down the mouse button on a vertical scroll bar arrow.
Move to the next or previous transaction or list item	Click on the arrows on a vertical scroll bar.
Page up or page down a screen	Click on either side of the scroll box.
Select options	Click on the option to switch between on and off.

Figure 1.5 shows the vertical scroll bar arrow and box on a register screen.

For the remainder of this book, the term *select* (for mouse users) will mean to point and click on the item.

Backing Up Your Data Files

Although Quicken automatically saves the data from your work session when you edit, it's wise to keep backup copies of all financial data. To make a backup of your data file before exiting Quicken, follow these steps:

1. Press Esc to return to the Main menu (if necessary).

2. Press Ctrl-E at the Main menu to access the backup option.

3. Place your backup disk in drive A or B.

4. Type the drive letter for your backup disk. Press Enter.

5. Quicken displays the list of Quicken data files. Select the file that you want to back up, and press Enter to begin the backup process.

Vertical scoll bar arrow

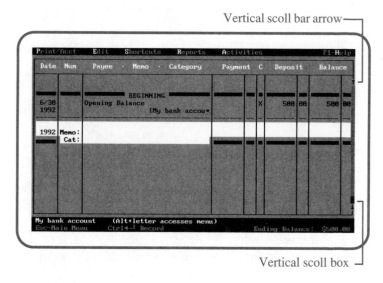

Vertical scoll box

Figure 1.5 The vertical scroll bar arrow and the vertical scroll box.

Backing Up Without Exiting   Press Ctrl-B from the Main menu to back up your files without exiting Quicken. Then follow the backup process.

Automatic Backup Reminders Quicken reminds you to back up your data at intervals that you specify. Each time you run Quicken, it gives you the options of being reminded weekly, or monthly. Select these options by setting preferences. (See Lesson 2 to learn how to set preferences.)

Exiting Quicken

To exit Quicken and automatically save your data files:

1. Press Esc to return to the Main menu (if necessary).

2. Press X to select Exit from the Main menu. Quicken saves your data files and returns you to the DOS prompt.

Unsaved Data If you turn your computer off before exiting Quicken through the Main menu, you may lose some of your data. Although Quicken reconstructs some files the next time it is used, complete reconstruction of data files is not possible.

   In the next lesson, you learn how to set up Quicken so that you can begin using the program.

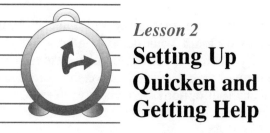

Lesson 2

Setting Up Quicken and Getting Help

In this lesson, you will learn how to set preferences (program options) and how to use Quicken's on-screen Help system.

Setting Preferences

Quicken allows you to customize the program to better fit your needs by setting preferences for items such as screen settings, printer settings, passwords, electronic payment settings, and more.

To set preferences, follow these steps:

1. Select Set Preferences from the Main menu.

2. Quicken displays the Set Preferences menu.

3. From the Set Preferences menu, select any of the options below which you want to activate:

   Printer Settings to assign printer settings for check printing and report printing (see Lesson 9).

Screen Settings to tell Quicken the type of monitor you are using and to set display options. Quicken 6 provides more screen colors and background patterns to choose from. You can also specify which type of menu you want to use, Alt-key or Function key.

Password Settings to assign file and transaction passwords.

Reminder Settings to turn Quicken's Billminder feature on or off and to specify the number of days in advance to be reminded of checks to print and transaction groups that are due.

Transaction Settings to provide instructions for handling transactions entered in Quicken. For example, if you want Quicken to request confirmation when a transaction is modified, you can choose this option from the Transaction Settings menu. You can also tell Quicken not to beep when recording transactions or performing amortization calculations.

Checks and Reports Settings to provide instructions for printing checks and reports. For example, if you want the category name printed on voucher checks, you can choose this option from the Checks and Reports Settings menu.

Electronic Payment Settings to set up Quicken to pay bills electronically through CheckFree.

Using Quicken with Windows   You can set up Quicken to work with Microsoft Windows 286, 386, 3.0, or 3.1 as a non-Windows application. (See your Quicken user manual for more information.)

Using Quicken's Help System

Quicken offers a fully indexed, topical Help system. With Quicken 6, you can get context-sensitive Help that allows you to access assistance for a particular field. To access a Quicken Help screen, follow these steps:

1. From anywhere in Quicken, press F1 or Alt-H. Quicken displays a window of information about the current screen.

2. If a topic, within the information window, is boldfaced or colored, you can move the cursor to the topic and press Enter to display an additional window of information related to that topic only. For example, in Figure 2.1, you see the Help window displayed from the Quicken Main menu. When you move the cursor to the Use Register line and press Enter, a screen is displayed with Help information about the Use Register command.

3. To remove the Help window from the screen, press Esc.

Move the cursor to a topic and press Enter to display additional help.

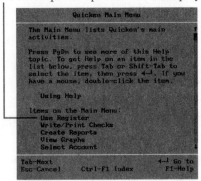

Figure 2.1   The Main menu Help screen.

Using the Help Index

Quicken's Help system is indexed by topic. To locate a topic using the Help index, follow these steps:

1. Press Ctrl-F1 from anywhere in Quicken.

2. Quicken displays the Help Index window shown in Figure 2.2.

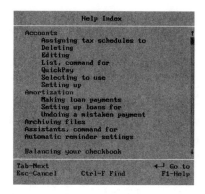

Figure 2.2　Topics listed in the Help Index window.

3. Move around the Help Index using the Up and Down Arrow keys, the PgDn and PgUp keys, or the Tab key.

4. Use the following keys to locate topics:

    Tab—moves to the next boldfaced or colored topic.

    Any **Alphabet key**—moves to the first topic that begins with that letter.

    Ctrl-F—displays the Find window in which you type a word or phrase to search.

    Backspace—returns to the Help message you just left.

5. When you've located the topic that you need help with, press Enter to display the Help screen for that topic.

Accessing the Help Table of Contents

Quicken's basic tasks are listed in a table of contents. To access the table of contents, follow these steps:

1. From anywhere in Quicken, press F1 twice.

2. Quicken displays a table of contents (see Figure 2.3) that you can use to select a task with which you need help.

Highlight a topic and press Enter for help. ——

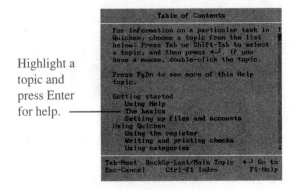

Figure 2.3 The Help Table of Contents listing Quicken's basic tasks.

3. Select the task that you need help with and press Enter to display the Help screen for that topic.

Getting Field-Specific Help

With Quicken 6.0, you can get help for fields in any Quicken screen or window with three or more date entry fields. To get help for a particular field, follow these steps:

1. Position the cursor on the field for which you want to see field-specific Help.

2. Press F1 or Alt-H. Quicken displays a help screen with information that pertains to that field only. Figure 2.4 shows the field-specific Help screen for the Date field in the Write Checks screen.

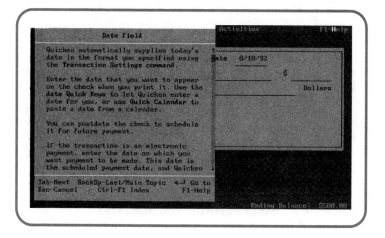

Figure 2.4 The field-specific Help screen for the Date field in the Write Checks screen.

Getting Screen Help From a field-specific Help screen, you can also get help for the entire screen where the field is located by pressing the Backspace key.

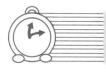

Using Tutorials and Assistants

Quicken 6's Tutorials and Assistants option provides you with an overview of the program and serves as an on-screen demonstration for first-time setup procedures. To use Tutorials and Assistants, follow these steps:

1. Select Use Tutorials/Assistants from the Main menu to display the Tutorials and Assistants menu.

2. Select from the following options:

   First Time **S**etUp if you are a new Quicken user and need help getting started.

   See Quicken **O**verview if you want a brief presentation on the program features.

   Create New **F**ile if you need help setting up a Quicken file.

   Create New **A**ccount if you want assistance in setting up an account.

   Create **P**ayroll Support if you want Quicken to set up payroll categories and accounts that you can use in your small business.

   Export Tax Information if you want help creating a file that you can import to TurboTax or another tax preparation program.

   More Assistants if you need assistance in amortizing a loan or to see an overview of Quicken's investment features.

3. Follow the on-screen prompts.

   In the next lesson, you will learn how to set up accounts in your Quicken file.

Lesson 3

Setting Up Accounts

In this lesson, you'll learn how to set up and select the accounts that you will use in Quicken.

Before you can start using Quicken to record transactions, you must set up the accounts that you will use to track your financial activity.

Accounts and Transactions An *account* is an individual record of financial transactions. *Transactions* increase or decrease the balance in any given account.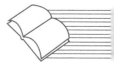

Types of Accounts

The following is a list of the six account types that you can use to track your financial activity. Each account description contains a reference to the lesson that teaches you about working with that account type.

- **Bank**. This is the most commonly used account type. It includes checking, savings, or money market accounts. (See Lesson 4.)

- **Credit Card**. These accounts keep track of your credit card transactions. (See Lesson 14.)

- **Cash**. Cash accounts keep track of your cash expenditures. (See Lesson 15.)

- **Other Asset**. Use this account type to record and track the value of things that you own, such as your home or auto.

- **Other Liability**. This account type records and tracks the debts that you owe, such as the mortgage on your home or the outstanding loan balance on your auto.

- **Investment**. Use this type to track investments such as stocks, bonds, and mutual funds. Because this account type represents one of Quicken's more advanced features, it will not be covered in this book. See your Quicken user manual for more information.

Setting Up an Account

To set up any one of the six Quicken account types:

1. Press A to choose Select Account from the Main menu or press Ctrl-A to display the Select Account to Use window.

2. Using the Up Arrow key, move the arrow to the <New Account> line in the Select Account to Use window (see Figure 3.1) and press Enter.

3. Quicken displays the Set Up New Account window as shown in Figure 3.2.

4. Type a number (see Figure 3.2) to select an account type.

5. Press Enter.

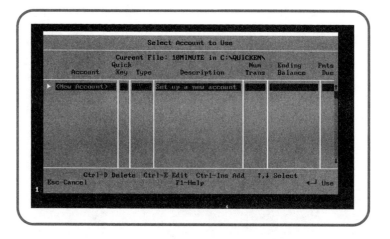

Figure 3.1 The Select Account to Use window.

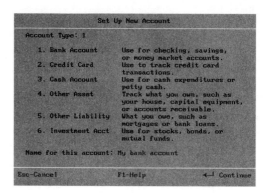

Figure 3.2 The Set Up New Account window.

6. Type the name for the account and press Enter. For example, if you are setting up a bank account, the account name you enter might be First National. Account names may be up to 15 characters in length and may include spaces, numbers, or other characters except [,] , / , and : .

7. Quicken displays the Starting Balance and Description window next (as shown in Figure 3.3). Enter the balance of your account and press Enter. You must make an entry in the Balance field, even if the balance is zero (in which case, you type 0).

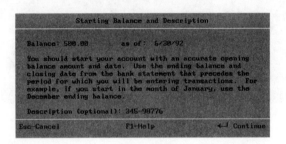

Figure 3.3 The Starting Balance and Description window.

Entering a Balance   For bank accounts, enter the ending balance as shown on your last bank statement. For credit card accounts, enter the balance due from your last statement. Enter the amount of cash on hand for cash accounts. For other asset accounts, enter the current value of the asset. For other liability accounts, enter the current principal portion, plus accrued interest, of the liability.

8. Type the date that relates to the balance entered in Step 7 and press Enter. (Note: You may override the default system date.)

Entering Dates   Press the + key to increase the date by one day; press the − key to decrease the date by one day. Press T to enter today's date.

20

9. Type a description of the account and press Enter. Descriptions are optional and may be up to 20 characters in length. Examples of descriptions you may want to use are the account number of your bank account or credit card, or the street address of real estate.

10. If you're setting up a bank account, Quicken displays the Source of Starting Balance window next. See Lesson 4 to learn how to fill in this window. If you're setting up a Credit Card Account, Quicken displays the Specify Credit Limit window next. See Lesson 14 to learn how to fill in this window.

The account that you have just set up is entered in the Select Account to Use window.

Selecting an Account to Use

Quicken records transactions in an electronic register for each account. Before you can write checks or enter transactions into a register, you must tell Quicken which account you want to use. To select an account, follow these steps:

1. Select Account from the Main menu or press Ctrl-A to display the Select Account to Use window.

2. Using the Up and Down Arrow keys, move the arrow to the account that you want to use in the Select Account to Use window and press Enter. Quicken accesses the register for the account that you select.

Electronic Register An *electronic register* is an on-screen register that lists the date and amount of a transaction, the payee, and the current balance in the account. Electronic registers are very similar to your manual check register.

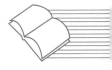

21

Selecting an Account To avoid scrolling through a long list of Quicken accounts, type the first letter of the account name that you want to select. Quicken highlights the first account name that begins with that letter.

Assigning Quick Keys to Accounts

Quicken enables you to assign your own Quick key to the accounts that you use most often. Using Quick keys, you can select an account from any screen by pressing the Ctrl key in combination with the Quick key that you assigned to the account. To assign a Quick key to an account:

1. Press A to choose Select Account from the Main menu or press Ctrl-A to display the Select Account to Use window.

2. Using the Up and Down Arrow keys, move the arrow to the account to which you want to assign a Quick key.

3. Press Ctrl-E to access the Edit Account Information window.

4. Assign a number from 1-9 in the Quick Key Assignment field.

5. Press Ctrl-Enter to record the Quick Key assignment.

Editing an Account

After you have set up an account, you can make changes to the account name and/or the account description. To edit an account:

1. Using the Up and Down Arrow keys, move the arrow to the account that you want to edit in the Select Account to Use window.

2. Press Ctrl-E to select the Edit option and display the Edit Account Information window.

3. Type over the account name and/or the account description.

4. Press Enter to save the changes to the account.

Deleting an Account

You can delete accounts from the Quicken account list. However, once deleted, the account is permanently removed and cannot be restored. To delete an account:

1. Using the Up and Down Arrow keys, move the arrow to the account that you want to delete in the Select Account to Use window.

2. Press Ctrl-D to select the Delete option.

3. Quicken displays a caution that a deleted account will be permanently removed. Type YES if you are sure that you want to delete the account.

4. Press Enter to delete the account.

In the next lesson, you'll learn how to work with a Quicken bank account.

Lesson 4

Working with Bank Accounts

In this lesson, you'll learn how to set up a bank account that you can use to write and print checks and/or enter other transactions such as deposits and ATM withdrawals.

Setting Up a Bank Account

A bank account is a Quicken account used to write and print checks. Bank accounts include checking, savings, or money market accounts. To set up a bank account (see Lesson 3 for more on setting up a new account), follow these steps:

1. In the Account Type field found in the Set Up New Account window, press 1 to select Bank Account and press Enter

2. Type the name of the account and press Enter. Usually, this will be the name of the bank and/or the type of bank account. For example, you might enter 1st Natl-Check to denote that the account is a checking account with First National Bank.

3. Quicken displays the Starting Balance and Description window shown in Figure 4.1. Type the starting balance in your account and press Enter. This is the ending balance from your last bank statement.

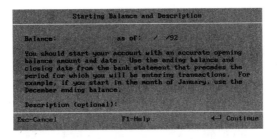

Figure 4.1 The Starting Balance and Description window for setting up a bank account.

The balance in your checking or savings register may be different than the balance that your bank shows in your account. Bank service charges and/or interest earned are usually debited or credited to your account on the date that your bank generates your statement. To accurately reflect your account balance, set up your Quicken bank account after receiving a statement from your bank, and enter the balance as shown on your statement. Remember to enter any uncleared transactions (that is, checks not cleared by the bank or deposits not credited to your account) in the Quicken check register. (See Lesson 5 to learn how to enter transactions into the check register.)

4. Type the date that relates to the starting balance that you entered in step 3 and press Enter. If you are using your last bank statement, enter the statement date.

5. Type a description (optional) of the account and press Enter. If you have more than one checking or savings account with the same bank, enter an account number here.

6. Quicken next displays the Source of Starting Balance window. Tell Quicken where you got your bank account starting balance by pressing 1 if you used the

25

ending balance from your bank statement, 2 if you used the balance from your check register, or 3 if you used some other source. Press Enter.

7. If you used your bank statement as the source of the starting balance in your bank account, Quicken displays a congratulatory message telling you that the bank statement is the most accurate source. Press Enter to add the bank account to your list of accounts in the Select Account to Use window. Figure 4.2 shows an example account added to the Select Account to Use window.

New bank account

			Select Account to Use			
			Current File: 10MINUTE in C:\QUICKEN\			
Account	Quick Key	Type	Description	Num Trans	Ending Balance	Pmts Due
<New Account>			Set up a new account			
My bank account		Bank	345-98776	1	500.00	

Ctrl-D Delete Ctrl-E Edit Ctrl-Ins Add ↑,↓ Select
Esc-Cancel F1-Help ↵ Use

Figure 4.2 The Select Account to Use window with a bank account added.

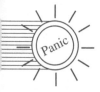

Check Register or Other Source Used? If you used the balance from your check register or some other source for your bank account starting balance, Quicken displays a message with Intuit's recommendation that you use your bank statement balance. To go back and re-enter your starting balance using your bank statement, press Y. To establish your starting balance using your check register or some other source, press N.

In the next lesson, you will learn how to enter transactions in the check register for your bank account.

Lesson 5

Using the Check Register

In this lesson, you'll learn how to use the Quicken check register to record all of the activity that affects your bank account balance.

Opening the Check Register

The Quicken check register is similar to a manual check register by the way it records all bank account activity.

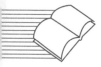

Check Register A *check register* pertains specifically to a bank account. The check register lists the date of a transaction, the check number, payee, payment amount, deposit amount, memo message (optional), category (optional), status of the transaction (whether it has cleared the bank), and the remaining balance in the account.

The check register is where you enter transactions for manual checks that you write. If you write checks at the Write Checks screen (see Lesson 8) using Quicken, your transactions are automatically recorded in the check register. Deposits, ATM withdrawals, adjustments, bank service charges, and interest earned on bank accounts are entered directly into the check register. Quicken adjusts your bank account balance for each transaction entered.

To access the Quicken check register:

1. Choose Select Account from the Main menu.

2. Select the bank account that you want to use. (See Lesson 3.)

3. Quicken displays the Check Register screen (Figure 5.1).

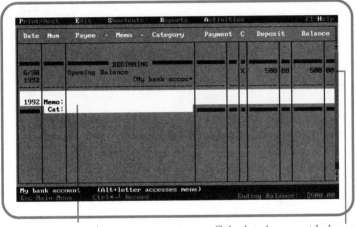

Enter new transactions in the highlighted area.

Calculated account balance after a transaction

Figure 5.1   The Check Register screen.

Quick Access   If you have already selected the bank account that you want to use and have performed another function (printed reports, written checks, etc.), open the check register by pressing Ctrl-R

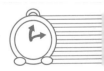

29

Entering Transactions into the Check Register

New transactions are entered in the blank transaction line at the end of the check register. To enter a transaction:

1. Access the bank account check register as described earlier in this lesson.

2. Enter the date, check number (if applicable), payee, payment or deposit amount, memo, and category. Press the Tab key or the Enter key to move to each field. Quicken 6's new QuickFill feature fills in transaction information for you. See "Using QuickFill" later in this lesson.

3. Press Ctrl-Enter or F10 to record the transaction.

Entry Shortcuts

You can quickly change a transaction date by pressing the + or – keys which move the date up or back. Press the + key to enter the next check number. You also use the + or – keys to change the check number. For example, if the check number shown is 1066, press the – key to change the check number to 1065. Quicken offers a few more options for quick entry in the Date field as follows:

Press T to change the date to today's date.

Press M to change the date to the first day of the current month.

Press H to change the date to the last day of the current month.

Press **Y** to change the date to the first day of the current year.

Press **R** to change the date to the last day of the current year.

Inserting Transactions   You can insert transactions anywhere in the register, not just at the end. Position the highlight bar on a transaction with the same date as the transaction that you want to enter and press Ctrl-Ins. Quicken sorts transactions in the register by date, therefore, when you insert a transaction and record it, Quicken automatically moves the transaction, if necessary, to its proper date order in the register.

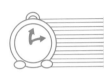

Copying and Pasting Transactions   You can copy an existing transaction in the register or the Write Checks screen and paste it (enter it) into another transaction line or blank check. Highlight the transaction or display the check that you want to copy and press Ctrl-Ins. Quicken memorizes the transaction. Then move to the transaction line or the blank check where you want to paste the transaction and press Shift-Ins.

Using QuickFill

QuickFill is Quicken 6's new feature that searches the last month's transactions in the register and the memorized transaction list to find a transaction that matches the first few characters that you type in the Payee field or the Category field in the register. When a matching transaction is found, QuickFill fills in the remaining fields in the transaction for you. You can tell QuickFill to keep looking if you want a different transaction. Note: You cannot use QuickFill to edit an existing transaction. To use QuickFill:

1. At the check register, enter the date and check number (if applicable) as usual.

2. In the Payee field, type the first few characters of the payee's name. QuickFill searches the last three months' transactions in the register and the memorized transaction list to find a transaction that begins with the characters you typed. When a matching transaction is found, QuickFill fills in the rest of the payee name and shows whether the transaction was found in the register (displayed as <MM/DD>) or the memorized transaction list (displayed as <MEM>).

3. If QuickFill enters the payee that you want, press Enter to accept it and QuickFill fills in the same payment or deposit amount, memo, and category from the matching transaction it found. If you don't want the payee that QuickFill entered, press Ctrl-+ or Ctrl-- (minus) to search forward or backward through the register or the memorized transaction list.

4. Record the transaction by pressing Ctrl-Enter or F10.

QuickFill Enters Categories QuickFill also works from the Category field. When you type the first few characters of the category name in the Category field, QuickFill searches the Category and Transfer List for the first category that begins with the characters that you type. QuickFill then enters the complete category name in the Category field. You can press Ctrl-+ or Ctrl-- (minus) to enter the next or last category from the list.

Finding Transactions in the Check Register

To quickly find a transaction without scrolling through the entire check register:

1. From the Check Register screen, press Alt-E to access the **E**dit pull-down menu and select Find, or just press Ctrl-F.

2. Type the information that matches the transaction that you are searching for in the Transaction to Find window shown in Figure 5.2. You can ask Quicken to find transactions that match payment or deposit amounts, payees, memos, or categories. If necessary, press Ctrl-D to clear the Transaction to Find window.

3. Press Ctrl-B to search backwards through the register or Ctrl-N to search forward. Continue pressing Ctrl-B or Ctrl-N until you have found the transaction that you are looking for.

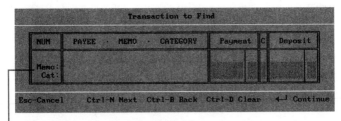

Enter information to help Quicken
find a transaction in the register.

Figure 5.2   The Transaction to Find window.

33

Unfound Transaction If you ask Quicken to search for a transaction and a message appears stating that no transaction was found, check to make sure you entered the information correctly in the Transaction to Find window.

Key Word Matches If you are unsure of the exact words or phrases used in the transaction you are trying to find, enter double periods (··) before or after a key word. For example, if you know that the name of a payee contains the word Market, type `market..` and Quicken will find transactions that begin with the word market, such as Market Research, Inc. or Market Developers, Inc.

Moving to a Specific Date

To find transactions in the check register that occurred on a specific date, follow these steps:

1. From the Check Register screen, press Alt-E to access the Edit pull-down menu and select Go to Date, or press Ctrl-G

2. Type the date in the Go to Date window or press the + or − keys to change the date forward or backwards.

3. Press Enter. Quicken finds the first transaction with the date that you entered in the Go to Date window.

Editing a Transaction in the Check Register

You can make changes to a transaction that you have entered in the check register. You cannot, however, edit or change the amount calculated in the remaining balance column of the check register. To edit a transaction:

1. Access the bank account check register, as explained earlier in this lesson.

2. Use the Up and Down Arrow keys, PgUp and PgDn keys, or the Home and End keys to move the highlight bar to the transaction that you want to edit.

3. Press the Tab or the Enter key to move to the field that you want to edit.

4. Make the necessary change(s) and press Ctrl-Enter or F10 to save the changes.

Deleting a Transaction from the Check Register

To delete a transaction from the check register:

1. Access the bank account check register.

2. Use the Up and Down Arrow keys, PgUp and PgDn keys, or the Home and End keys to move the highlight bar to the transaction that you want to delete.

3. Press Alt-E to access the **E**dit pull-down menu and select Delete Transaction, or just press Ctrl-D.

4. At the OK to Delete Transaction window, press 1 to select Delete Transaction and remove the transaction from the check register. (Note: If you have set the transaction setting for confirming deleted or voided transactions to N (No), Quicken will not display the OK to Delete Transaction window; the transaction will be deleted immediately after you select Delete Transaction. See Lesson 2 for more on transaction settings.)

In the next lesson, you'll learn how to use the program calculator and calendar.

Lesson 6

Using the Calculator and the Calendar

In this lesson, you'll learn how to use Quicken's on-screen calculator and the new calendar feature called Quick Calendar.

Accessing the Calculator

To access the Quicken calculator, follow these steps:

1. From the Write Checks screen or any register screen, press Alt-A to access the Activities pull-down menu.

2. To select Calculator, press C to display the Quicken calculator (shown in Figure 6.1).

Quick Access You can access the on-screen calculator at any time in Quicken simply by pressing Ctrl-O.

Using the Calculator

The on-screen calculator adds, subtracts, multiplies, and divides numbers. To use the calculator, follow these steps:

1. Access the Quicken calculator, as explained earlier in this lesson.

2. Enter the first number in your calculation. What you enter appears in the cursor line until you press an arithmetic sign or Enter.

3. Press one of the following:

   +   to add a number.

   −   to subtract a number.

   /   to divide a number.

   *   to multiply a number.

4. Enter the other numbers and arithmetic signs to continue your calculation.

5. Press Enter to total your calculation.

Click the calculator's keypad
with the mouse.

Figure 6.1 The Quicken calculator.

Chain Calculations   After you have pressed Enter, you can enter the last calculated total into a
subsequent calculation by pressing + or *. Quicken
will enter the last calculated total as the first number
in your next calculation.

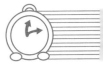

Clearing the Calculator   To clear the last calculation from the calculator, press C to select **Clear**.

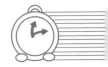

Using Percentages

To add or subtract a percentage from a number, follow these
steps:

1. Enter the number that you want to add a percentage to
   or subtract a percentage from.

2. Press + to add or – to subtract.

3. Enter the percentage that you want to add or subtract.

4. Press % to convert the last number entered to a percentage.

5. Press Enter to calculate the total.

Pasting (Copying) Calculations

Using the Paste feature, you can enter the calculated amount
from the on-screen calculator into an amount field in the
Quicken program. To paste or copy a calculated amount
into Quicken, follow these steps:

1. Position the cursor on the Amount field to which you want to copy a calculated number.

2. Press Ctrl-O to access the Quicken calculator.

3. Perform your calculation.

4. To copy the calculated amount to the amount field, press F9 to select Paste.

After you paste an amount to the amount field, Quicken clears the calculator from the screen.

Closing the Calculator

When you finish using the calculator, simply press Esc to clear the screen. The last calculation performed will appear the next time you access the calculator.

Using Quicken's On-Screen Calendar

A new feature in Quicken 6 is Quick Calendar which is an on-screen calendar that you can use to review dates, to enter or paste a date in the Date field of the Register or the Write Checks screen, or to find a specific transaction.

Accessing Quick Calendar

To access the Quicken calendar, follow these steps:

1. From the Write Checks screen or any register screen, press Alt-A to access the **Activities** pull-down menu.

2. Press A to select Calendar to display Quick Calendar (shown in Figure 6.2). When you first access Quick Calendar, the current date is highlighted.

The current
date is
highlighted.

```
                  Quick Calendar
                  August - 1992
        Sun   Mon   Tue   Wed   Thur  Fri   Sat
                                             1
        2     3     4     5     6     7     8
        9     10    11    12    13    14    15
        16    17    18    19    20    21    22
        23    24    25    26    27    28    29
        30    31    first day: Month  Year  Today
                    last day:  montH  yeaR
         PgUp,PgDn-Month      F9-Paste Date
      Esc-Cancel      F1-Help  ◄─┘ Go to Date
```

Figure 6.2   The Quicken Quick Calendar.

Quick Access   You can access Quick Calendar from any register or the Write Checks screen simply by pressing Ctrl-K.

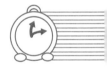

Selecting Dates in Quick Calendar   To select a date in the current month, use the up, down, right, and left arrow keys. To change the month, use the PgUp key to move back one month or the PgDn key to move forward a month. To quickly select a date, press T for today's date, M for the first day of the current month, Y for the first day of the current year, H for the last day of the current month, or R for the last day of the current year.

Finding Transactions Using Quick Calendar

To find a transaction in the register or the Write Checks screen using Quick Calendar, follow these steps:

41

1. From the Register or the Write Checks screen, press Ctrl-K to access Quick Calendar.

2. Select the date of the transaction that you're looking for.

3. Press Enter. Quicken goes to the first transaction in the Register or the Write Checks screen with that date.

Pasting (Entering) Dates from Quick Calendar

To enter or paste a date in a date field, follow these steps:

1. Position the cursor on the Date field into which you want to paste a date.

2. Press Ctrl-K to access Quick Calendar.

3. Select the date that you want to enter in the Date field.

4. To select Paste Date, press F9 to enter the selected date in the Amount field and remove Quick Calendar from the screen.

Removing Quick Calendar

To exit Quick Calendar and remove it from the screen, press Esc. Quicken returns to the register or screen that you were working in before you accessed Quick Calendar.

In the next lesson, you'll learn how to set up and assign categories to transactions.

Lesson 7

Setting Up and Assigning Categories

In this lesson, you'll learn how to set up and assign categories to transactions.

Setting Up Categories

Quicken includes preset, standard home and business categories. You choose which category list (home or business) you want to use when you set up your first Quicken file during installation, or when you set up additional files. (See Lesson 22.) You can add, edit, or delete categories from the standard lists. Quicken stores the categories that you use in the Category and Transfer List.

Category *Categories* are groupings of income and expenses; they are used to classify your transactions for budgeting and income tax reporting purposes. For example, you may categorize your expenses into the following groups: rent, utilities, groceries, medical, entertainment, and so on.

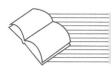

Adding a Category

To add a new category, follow these steps:

1. From the Write Checks screen or any register screen, select the Shortcuts pull-down menu and select Categorize/Transfer, or just press Ctrl-C. Quicken displays the Category and Transfer List as shown in Figure 7.1.

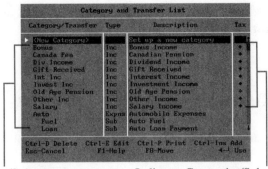

Category/Subcategory names   Indicates Categories/Subcategories
that are tax-related.

Figure 7.1   The Category and Transfer List.

2. Press Home to move to the <New Category> line and press Enter. Quicken displays the Set Up Category window as seen in Figure 7.2.

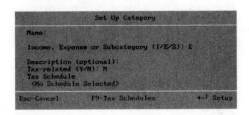

Figure 7.2   Use the Set Up Category window to add a new category.

3. Type the name of the category and press Enter. Category names can be up to 15 characters (including spaces), but cannot include : / [ ].

4. Press one of the following:

   I   for income categories.

   E   for expenses categories.

   S   for subcategories.

Subcategory A *subcategory* further divides a category into a secondary category. For example, you might divide a medical category by setting up subcategories like hospital, doctor, drugs, and so on.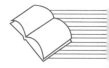

5. Type a category description and press Enter. (Note: Category descriptions appear in report headings.)

Category Names If you prefer to have the category names appear on your reports instead of the category descriptions, change the checks and reports setting from the Set Preferences menu. (See Lesson 2 to learn more about how to change checks and reports settings.)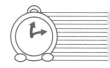

6. Type Y if the category is tax-related. All categories designated as tax-related will appear on the Personal Tax Summary Report.

7. If you want to assign a tax schedule to this category, press F9. Quicken displays the Tax Schedule window. Position the highlight bar on the tax schedule for this category and press Enter. Next Quicken displays the

Tax Line window. Scroll through the window to select the description of the tax line for this category and press Enter. If Quicken provides more than one copy of the tax schedule that you select (for example, Schedule C or Form W-2), the Schedule Copy Number is displayed next so that you can enter the number of the copy where you want the category data entered in the Personal Tax Summary Report. (Note: You cannot edit the Tax Schedule field directly; you must access the Tax Schedules window by pressing F9.)

8. Press F10 to add the new category to the Category and Transfer List.

Adding Categories While Entering Transactions   You can add a new category from the Write Checks screen or any register screen while you are entering transactions. When you type a category name in the Category field that is not included in the Category and Transfer List (because it's new), Quicken displays the Category Not Found window. Press 1 to add the category that you just entered to the list, then follow the steps just explained to add a new category.

Using Tax Schedules   Quicken lets you assign a tax schedule to each category. Then, at the end of the year, you can run a Tax Schedule report to summarize all of your transactions by tax schedule. If you prepare your own income taxes, this feature will give you everything you need to transfer amounts to the related tax form or schedule. For example, Dividend Income is reported on Schedule B of Form 1040. You can assign the Dividend Income category to Schedule B and at the end of the year, all transactions assigned to the Dividend Income category will appear under the Schedule B heading of the Tax Schedule report.

Editing a Category

Quicken enables you to make changes to existing categories. To edit a category:

1. Select Categorize/Transfer from the Shortcuts pull-down menu, or press Ctrl-C to access the Category and Transfer List.

2. Move the arrow to the category that you want to edit.

3. Press Ctrl-E to access the Edit Category window.

4. Make the necessary changes to the Edit Category window.

5. Press Ctrl-Enter or F10 to save the changes.

Deleting a Category

You can delete categories from the Category and Transfer List at any time. To delete a category:

1. Select the Categorize/Transfer option from the Shortcuts pull-down menu or press Ctrl-C to access the Category and Transfer List.

2. Move the arrow to the category that you want to delete.

3. Press Ctrl-D to select the **D**elete option.

4. Quicken displays a warning stating that you are about to permanently delete a category.

5. Press Enter to delete the category.

Changing Categories and Subcategories You can change a category to a subcategory (or vice versa), or move a subcategory to another category. From the Category and Transfer List, highlight the category or subcategory that you want to change or move and press F8. Then use the arrow keys to move the category or subcategory where you want it in the Category and Transfer List.

Merging Categories You can merge one category into another category. For example, you may want to merge the *Interest Income* category into the *Investment Income* category if you find that you are not really using the former category. Highlight the category and then change it to a subcategory (as explained in the previous tip). Highlight the new subcategory and press Ctrl-D to delete the new subcategory from the list.

Printing the Category List

You may want a hard copy of the categories that you have set up to use with Quicken. Before you print, make sure that Quicken is set up for your printer. To set up Quicken to print reports, follow the steps for setting up Quicken to print checks (in Lesson 9) but select the Settings for Printing Reports option instead. To print the Category and Transfer List:

1. Select Categorize/Transfer from the Shortcuts pull-down menu, or press Ctrl-C to access the Category and Transfer List.

2. Press Ctrl-P to select the Print option.

3. Type the number of the printer that you are using if it is different than the default.

4. Press Enter to print the Category and Transfer List.

Assigning Categories to Transactions

You can assign categories to transactions to help track your income and expenses. Assigning categories is optional; Quicken does not require an entry in the Category field. To assign a category to a transaction:

1. Press Ctrl-R to access the check register as explained in Lesson 5. (Note: Categories can also be assigned to transactions from the Write Checks screen. See Lesson 8.)

2. Enter the transaction information: date, check number, payee, payment or deposit amount, and memo.

3. Type the category name in the Category field. You can type the category name in either uppercase or lowercase, regardless of how it was set up in the Category and Transfer List. To assign a subcategory, type : after the category name and then type the subcategory name. (Note: Quicken checks the category/subcategory name that you enter to see if it is in the Category and Transfer List. If not, Quicken gives you the option of selecting

49

another category from the list or creating the new category that you just typed.)

4. Press Ctrl-Enter or F10 to record the transaction.

Using QuickFill to Assign Categories   You can use Quicken's new QuickFill feature to assign a category to a transaction quickly and easily. Just type the first few characters of the category name and QuickFill searches the Category and Transfer List and enters the first category name that begins with the characters that you type. See Lesson 5 for more on QuickFill.

Assigning Categories from the Category List   If you aren't sure which category/subcategory you want to assign to a transaction, you can browse through the Category and Transfer List and select the category directly from the list. Press Ctrl-C to display the list. Highlight the category you want, and press Enter to assign it.

Using Classes   A class specifies who, where, or what time period a transaction is related to. Classes are an extension of categories. For example, if you own a number of apartment buildings, you might want to set up a class for each building to track the amount of income and expenses that relate to each property. To set up a class, press Ctrl-L, then highlight the <New Class> line and press Enter, and then fill in the class name and description. To assign a class to a transaction, type a colon (:) after the category name in the Category field, press Ctrl-L to display the Class List, and select the class from the list. You can also edit or delete classes from the Class List by pressing Ctrl-E or Ctrl-D.

Transfer Transactions   You can assign another Quicken account to a transaction by entering the account in the Category field. This is called a *transfer transaction.* In effect, a transfer transaction transfers funds from one account (say your checking account) to another account (say your savings account). When you assign an account to a transaction, Quicken automatically creates the corresponding transaction in that account. If you want to see the corresponding transfer transaction, highlight the transaction in the register and press Ctrl-X.

In the next lesson, you'll learn how to write checks.

Lesson 8

Writing
Checks

In this lesson, you will learn how to use Quicken to
write checks.

Writing Checks

Checks that you want to print using Quicken are written at
the Write Checks screen. Checks that you write are not
printed until you tell Quicken to print checks. (See Lesson
9 to learn how to print checks).

The Write Checks screen is similar to a blank check.
(Note: Checks written by hand are not entered in the Write
Checks screen. Manual checks, deposits, and bank fees are
entered in the check register. See Lesson 5 for more
information on entering manual transactions.) To write a
check in the Write Checks screen:

1. Select Write/Print Checks from the Main menu. Or, at
   the check register select Write Checks from the Activities pull-down menu or press Ctrl-W. Quicken displays
   the Write Checks screen as shown in Figure 8.1. (Note:
   Quicken checks are prenumbered so you do not enter a
   check number in this screen.)

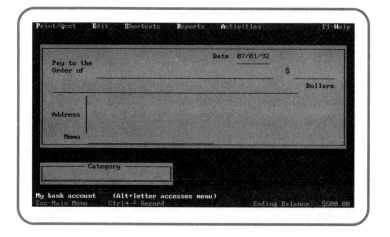

Figure 8.1 Writing a check at the Write Checks screen.

2. Type the date of the check and press Enter. (Note: Quicken automatically enters the current date; however, you can enter any date in the check's Date field.)

Changing Dates   To quickly change the date in the Write Checks screen, press + to increase the date one day at a time, or press − to decrease the date one day at a time.

3. Type the payee's name. Quicken's new QuickFill feature searches the last three months' transactions in the register and the memorized transaction list to find a payee that matches the first few characters that you type in the Payee field. When QuickFill finds a matching payee, the complete payee name is filled in for you. To accept the payee, press Enter and QuickFill enters the

rest of the transaction (payment or deposit amount, memo, and category) from the matching transaction. If you don't want to accept the payee that QuickFill enters, press Ctrl-+ to search forwards or Ctrl-- (minus) to search backwards.

4. Type the amount of the check and press Enter. The maximum amount for any check is $9,999,999.99. Quicken automatically enters the written dollar amount.

5. If you are using window envelopes to mail your checks, type ' in the first address line to copy the payee's name. Type the address in the remaining four lines and press Enter.

6. Type a memo for this check (optional) and press Enter.

7. If you want to assign a category, class, and/or subclass to this transaction, type the appropriate names in the Category field. (See Lessons 7 and 10 for more on assigning categories and/or classes to transactions.)

8. Press Ctrl-Enter or F10 to record the check.

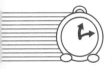

Memorized Transactions   If you write the same checks on a regular basis, you can memorize a check and recall it later so that you don't have to enter the same information each time.

Writing Postdated Checks

You can write all of your checks at one time and type a future date (postdate) at the Write Checks screen. Then, as a postdated check becomes due, simply tell Quicken to print the check. Postdated checks are separated from current or past checks by a double-line in the check register and appear with the date highlighted. Quicken calculates the total amount of unprinted checks so that you know exactly how much you will need to cover all postdated checks. The Checks to Print total appears in the lower right corner of the Write Checks screen.

Reviewing and Editing Checks

Before you print a check, you should review (and edit, if necessary) the check. You can review and make changes to checks in the check register or at the Write Checks screen. To review and edit a check at the Write Checks screen:

1. Select Write/Print Checks from the Main menu. Or, at the check register select Write Checks from the Activities pull-down menu or press Ctrl-W. Quicken displays the Write Checks screen.

2. Scroll through the checks using:

   PgUp to review the preceding check.

   PgDn to review the next check.

   Ctrl-Home to review the first check.

   Ctrl-End and **PgUp** to review the last check.

3. Review the check and make any necessary changes by typing over the entries in the Write Checks screen.

4. Press Ctrl-Enter or F10 to record the changes or Esc to cancel the changes.

5. Quicken automatically displays the next check.

Finding Checks You can use the Find (Ctrl-F) and Go to Date (Ctrl-G) features of Quicken to locate a check (see Lesson 5).

Deleting a Check

You can delete checks you have written, but not printed, at any time. Checks can be deleted from the Write Checks screen or the check register. To delete a check from the Write Checks screen:

1. Select Write/Print Checks from the Main menu. Or, if you are at the check register, select Write Checks from the Activities pull-down menu or press Ctrl-W. Quicken displays the Write Checks screen.

2. Use the PgUp, PgDn, Ctrl-Home, or Ctrl-End keys to display the check that you want to delete.

3. Select Delete Transaction from the Edit pull-down menu or press Ctrl-D.

4. Quicken displays the OK to Delete Transaction window shown in Figure 8.2.

5. Press 1 to delete the check.

Voiding a Check

You can *void* (cancel) a check that you have written using Quicken. Checks are voided in the check register, not the Write Checks screen. To void a check in the check register:

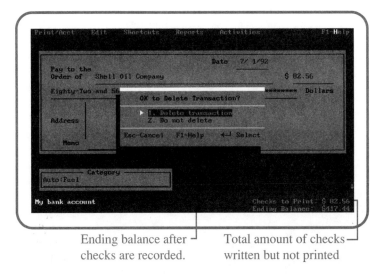

Ending balance after ⅃   Total amount of checks ⅃
checks are recorded.   written but not printed

Figure 8.2 The OK to Delete Transaction window
to delete a check.

1. Press Ctrl-R to access the check register.

2. Use the Up and Down Arrow keys or the Find (Ctrl-F)
   and Go to Date (Ctrl-G) features to highlight the check
   that you want to void.

3. Select Void Transaction from the Edit pull-down menu
   or press Ctrl-V.

4. Press 1 to void the transaction.

5. Quicken enters the word VOID before the payee name in
   the check register, and marks the transaction with an X
   to show that it is cleared and should not be included in
   the next bank reconciliation.

   The next lesson will show you how to print checks.

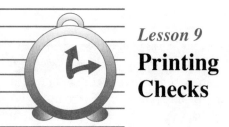

Lesson 9

Printing
Checks

In this lesson, you will learn how to print checks using Quicken.

Order checks from Intuit, publisher of Quicken, or any check printer that offers checks for use with Quicken. Quicken checks come in three different styles:

- Regular checks (3.5" high).

- Voucher checks (3.5" high, with a 3.5" perforated voucher below the check).

- Wallet checks (2 5/6" high, with a stub on the left).

    There are also two different check formats available:

- Continuous checks for use in continuous form printers.

- Laser checks that are grouped three to a page for regular checks, or one to a page for voucher checks.

Using Quicken's Interactive Order Form   With Quicken 6, you can display an Intuit product order form on-screen, fill in the order form, and print it to mail to Intuit. To display the order form, select the Order Supplies option from the Activities pull-down menu.

Assigning Printer Settings

Before you can start printing checks, you must tell Quicken what kind of printer you are using by assigning printer settings, as follows:

1. Select Set Preferences from the Main menu and then select Printer Settings, or just select Change Printer Styles from the Print/Acct pull-down menu.

2. Select the Settings for Printing Checks option. If you're assigning printer settings for reports, select the Settings for Printing Reports option or the Alternate Settings for Reports option.

3. Quicken displays the Style window and the Select Check Printer window overlaid on the Check Printer Settings window. Press Esc to remove the Style window so that you can select a printer from the printer list.

4. Highlight the name of your printer and press Enter to redisplay the Style window for your printer.

5. Highlight the style of print that you want for your checks and press Enter.

6. Quicken displays the Check Printer Settings window.

7. Make any necessary changes to the Check Printer Settings window and press Enter.

Printer Settings Quicken automatically enters the printer settings based on the printer that you select from the Printer List. Most of the time, these settings will be correct and no changes will need to be made to the Check Printer Settings window.

Positioning Checks in Your Printer

You can use a continuous form printer or a laser printer to print your checks. Print sample checks first to properly set alignment. If you're using a continuous form printer, use the sample checks enclosed in your Quicken package to print a sample check. If you're using a laser printer, print a sample check on plain paper.

To position checks in a continuous form printer:

1. Insert the sample checks into your printer (as you would continuous form paper) and turn on your printer. Make sure that you have at least one check to print before you continue with the next step.

2. Select Write/Print Checks from the Main menu or press Ctrl-W at the register to show the Write Checks screen.

3. Select Print Checks from the Print/Acct pull-down menu or just press Ctrl-P.

4. Quicken displays the Print Checks window. Type the number of the printer to print to and the number for the type of check that you are using.

5. Press F9 to print a sample check.

6. Review the sample check. If the sample check did not print correctly, type the position number to which the arrow for the pointer line is pointing and press Enter.

Pointer Line   A *pointer line* is the mark on the sample check that indicates where Quicken will start printing.

7. Quicken prints another sample check. Review the check. Repeat Step 6 as many times as needed to correctly print the sample check. If the horizontal adjustment of the print is off, move the checks in your printer to the right or left.

8. Press Enter when the sample check is printed correctly. Note the pointer line position and record it somewhere for future positioning. Also, note how the checks are aligned horizontally and make note of their placement for positioning checks in the future.

   To position checks for use with a laser printer:

1. Insert plain paper in your laser printer tray and turn on your printer. Make sure that you have at least one check to print before you print a sample check.

2. Make sure that the Page-Oriented Printer setting in the Check Printer Settings window is set to Y. Refer to the previous section to learn how to change printer settings.

3. Select Write/Print Checks from the Main menu or press Ctrl-W from the register to access the Write Checks screen.

4. Select Print Checks from the Print/Acct pull-down menu or just press Ctrl-P.

5. Quicken displays the Print Checks window. Type the number of the printer to print to, and the number for the type of check that you are using and press Ctrl-Enter.

6. Press Enter at the Enter Check Number window (don't worry about check numbers yet). Quicken prints the check information on a blank page.

7. Position the printed page over a sheet of preprinted laser checks and examine the alignment. If the print is properly aligned, press Enter at the Did Check Print Correctly? window to tell Quicken that the check printed correctly. You can skip the remaining steps.

8. Select No at the Did Check Print Correctly? window if the check did not print properly. When Quicken returns to the Print Checks window, press Ctrl-Enter and then press F7 to display the Vertical Check Adjustment window shown in Figure 9.1.

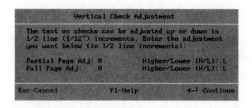

Figure 9.1 The Vertical Check Adjustment window.

9. Enter the number of 1/2 lines that you want to adjust the text on the check and then press H if you want the text adjusted higher on the check, or L if you want the text adjusted lower.

10. Press Ctrl-Enter to return to the Enter Check Number window and press Enter to print the second sample laser check.

11. Repeat steps 7 through 10 until the print is properly aligned.

Printing Checks

To print checks, follow these steps:

1. Turn on your printer and make sure that it is on-line.

2. Select Write/Print Checks from the Main menu or press Ctrl-W from the register to access the Write Checks screen.

3. Select Print Checks from the Print/Acct pull-down menu or just press Ctrl-P.

4. Quicken displays the Print Checks window as shown in Figure 9.2.

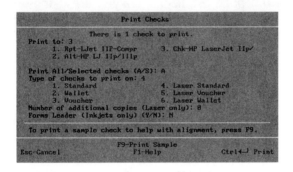

Figure 9.2 The Print Checks window.

5. Type the number of the printer that you want to use:

   1   for Report Printer

   2   for Alt Report Printer

   3   for Check Printer

6. Press Enter.

7. Tell Quicken which checks to print by pressing one of the following:

   A   to print all checks

   S   to print only selected checks

8. Type the number for the type of check that you are using and press Enter. (Note: You will not have to select the check type each time. Quicken will recall the check type the next time that you print checks.)

9. If you are using a laser printer, type the number of additional copies (up to three) that you want to print on a partial page of checks. (If you are using an inkjet printer, indicate whether you are using a laser forms leader.)

10. Press Ctrl-Enter.

11. If you typed an S to select the Selected Checks option in the Print Checks window, Quicken displays the Select Checks to Print window, shown in Figure 9.3. Use the Arrow keys to highlight each check that you want to print and press the Spacebar to select/deselect a check to print. Press F9 to select all checks. Press Enter when you have selected the checks.

12. At the Enter Check Number window, type the next blank check number if the number shown is not correct.

Changing Check Numbers To quickly change the check number in the Enter Check Number window, press + to increase the check number by one, or – to decrease the check number by one.

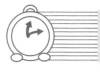

13. Press Enter to begin printing checks. (Quicken will ask you if your check(s) printed correctly. Press 1 for Yes and 2 for No.)

Indicates which
checks to print

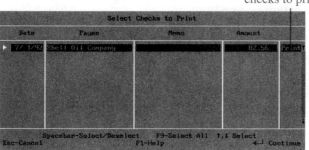

Figure 9.3 The Select Checks to Print window displays which checks you want printed.

Incorrectly Printed Checks Be sure to review all printed checks before you mail them. If a check is incorrect, you may reprint the check.

Reprinting Incorrectly Printed Checks You can reprint a check that did not print correctly by locating the check in the check register and replacing the entry in the Num (Check Number) field with an asterisk (*). Quicken changes the entry to a row of asterisks. Make any other necessary changes to the check transaction and press Ctrl-Enter or F10 to record the changes. Then access the Write Checks screen and print the check as explained above.

In the next lesson, you learn how to assign more than one category to a transaction.

Lesson 10

Working with Split Transactions

In this lesson, you will learn how to assign more than one category to a transaction by splitting the transaction.

Splitting Transactions

You can assign more than one category to a transaction, called splitting the transaction. For example, if you withdraw cash to pay for an evening out, you may want to assign three categories (Dining, Entertainment, and Sitter) to the transaction. To split a transaction:

1. From the Main menu, press Ctrl-R to access the check register as explained in Lesson 5. (You can also split transactions in the Write Checks screen. See Lesson 8.)

2. Enter all transaction information and the amount of the transaction into the register.

3. With the highlight bar on the transaction, select Split Transaction from the Edit pull-down menu, or press Ctrl-S to open the Split Transaction window as shown in Figure 10.1.

Type categories here.

Enter the amount for each category here.

Figure 10.1 You can assign more than one category to a transaction in the Split Transaction window.

4. Type the first category name and press Enter.

5. Type a description (optional) and press Enter.

6. Type the amount to be allocated to the first category and press Enter. (Note: You can enter positive or negative amounts in the Amount field.)

7. Continue entering categories, descriptions, and amounts until the total amount of the transaction is allocated to categories.

8. Press Ctrl-Enter or F10 to finish the split transaction.

9. Quicken returns to the register and enters SPLIT in the Check Number field as seen in Figure 10.2. In the Write Checks screen, Quicken enters SPLIT below the Category field. (Note: The word SPLIT does not appear on the printed check.)

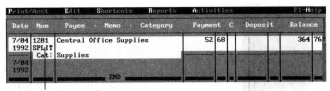

The register shows when
a transaction is split.

Figure 10.2   A split transaction noted in the
register.

10. Press Ctrl-Enter or F10 to record the split transaction.

Calculating Split Transactions   As you enter
each line of a split transaction, Quicken calculates
the remaining balance of the transaction and enters
the result in the next category line.

Copying in the Split Transaction Window   To
copy the main category name from the previous
line, type " in the Category field on the next line
and press Enter.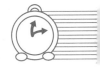

Splitting Transactions by Percentages

You can allocate percentages to split transactions. For
example, you may want to allocate an expense between
your business and home by percentage: 60% business and
40% home. To split transactions by percentages, follow
these steps:

1. Follow the steps just explained to open the Split Transaction window for a transaction.

69

2. Type the category name and memo (optional).

3. Type the percentage in the Amount field. Percentages are entered as 00%. For example, twenty percent is entered as 20%.

4. Press Enter and Quicken multiplies the transaction amount by the percentage and enters the result.

5. Repeat steps 2 through 4 to split the transaction further.

Editing Split Transactions

You can change the information in a split transaction. To edit a split transaction, follow these steps:

1. Position the highlight bar on the split transaction in the register that you want to edit.

2. Select Split Transaction from the Edit pull-down menu or press Ctrl-S to access the Split Transaction window.

3. Make any necessary changes to the Split Transaction window.

4. Press Ctrl-Enter or F10 to record the changes.

Eliminating Splits To delete a line in a split transaction, position the cursor on the line that you want to delete in the Split Transaction window and press Ctrl-D. To delete an entire split transaction, you must delete each line from the Split Transaction window and then press Ctrl-Enter.

Recalculating Split Transaction Amounts

If you enter an amount in the register or Write Checks screen for a transaction, you can recalculate the transaction amount using the Split Transaction window. To recalculate the amount, follow these steps:

1. Select Split Transaction from the Edit pull-down menu, or press Ctrl-S to open the Split Transaction window for a transaction.

2. Type the amounts in the Amount column. To subtract, enter a - (minus sign) before the amount.

3. After you have entered the amounts that make up the transaction amount, press F9 to select Recalc Transaction Total.

4. Quicken recalculates the transaction total and enters the result in the register as the transaction amount.

In the next lesson, you'll learn how to have Quicken recall transactions.

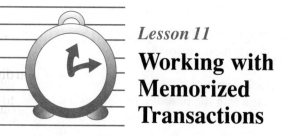

Lesson 11

Working with Memorized Transactions

In this lesson, you will learn how to have Quicken memorize and recall transactions.

You can quickly record your transactions in the check register, the Write Checks screen (see Lesson 8), or any other Quicken account register by using Quicken to memorize the transaction and later recall the transaction.

A *memorized transaction* is information saved from one transaction to be recalled for later transactions. They are transactions that you frequently record to the same payee, in the same amount, or allocated to the same income or expense category. Paychecks, mortgage payments, and car loan payments are examples of transactions that you may want to memorize.

Memorizing a Transaction

To memorize a transaction:

1. Type the transaction information that you want to memorize. (Note: You can enter and memorize any part of a transaction; you do not have to memorize a complete transaction.)

2. Select Memorize Transaction from the Shortcuts pull-down menu or press Ctrl-M.

3. Quicken highlights the information and displays a message that the marked information is about to be memorized. Press Enter to memorize the transaction.

Memorizing Recorded Transactions   You can memorize transactions that have already been recorded in the register. Just highlight the transaction that you want to memorize and press Ctrl-M. Quicken memorizes the entire transaction except the date and the check number.

(Note: Quicken keeps two lists of memorized transactions; one for noninvestment accounts and one for investment accounts. You cannot recall a memorized, noninvestment account transaction to an investment account register and vice versa.)

Recalling a Memorized Transaction

Once you have memorized a transaction, you can recall the transaction and record it in the Write Checks screen or any noninvestment Quicken register. To recall a memorized transaction:

1. At the Write Checks screen or in any Quicken non-investment account register, select Recall Transaction from the Shortcuts pull-down menu or press Ctrl-T. (Note: If the transaction that you want to recall is a check to be printed, you must recall the transaction at the Write Checks screen.)

2. Quicken displays the Memorized Transaction List.

3. Scroll through the Memorized Transaction List (see Figure 11.1) using the Up and Down Arrow keys. Position the arrow on the transaction that you want to recall and press Enter.

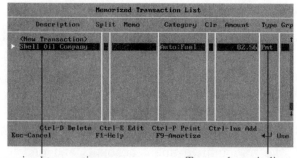

Memorized transaction   Type column indicates a
                                         payment, deposit, or check.

Figure 11.1   The Memorized Transaction List.

4. To add information to the recalled transaction, continue typing information to complete the transaction.

5. Press Ctrl-Enter or F10 to record the transaction.

Using QuickFill to Recall Transactions   To quickly recall a memorized transaction, type the first few letters of the payee name in the Payee field. QuickFill automatically searches the memorized transaction list or the last three months' transactions in the register for a matching payee and fills in the rest of the payee name. If the payee is the one that you want to enter, press Enter and QuickFill fills in the rest of the transaction. If the payee name that QuickFill enters is not the one you want, press

Ctrl-+ or Ctrl– (minus) to enter the previous or next payee from the memorized transaction list or the register. Quicken fills in the rest of the memorized transaction. See Lesson 5 for more on QuickFill.

Adding a Transaction to the Memorized Transaction List

You can add a memorized transaction directly to the Memorized Transaction List. To add a memorized transaction, follow these steps:

1. Select Recall Transaction from the Shortcuts pull-down menu or press Ctrl-T to access the Memorized Transaction List.

2. Press Home to highlight the <New Transaction> line.

3. Press Enter to access the Edit/Set Up Memorized Transaction window shown in Figure 11.2.

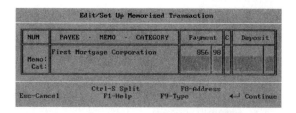

Figure 11.2   Adding a memorized transaction.

4. Type the transaction information in the Edit/Set Up Memorized Transaction window. (Note: You can open the Split Transaction window from this window to allocate the transaction to more than one category.)

5. Press F10 to add the transaction to the Memorized Transaction List.

Memorizing Addresses From the Edit/Set Up Memorized Transaction window, press F8 to memorize the address of the payee in a memorized transaction. Each time you recall the memorized transaction at the Write Checks screen, the memorized address will be filled in automatically.

Memorizing Deposit Transactions From the Edit/Set Up Memorized Transaction window, press F9 to designate a new memorized transaction as a deposit transaction. Quicken allows you to memorize a deposit transaction with a 0.00 amount.

Editing a Memorized Transaction

You can edit memorized transactions directly from the Memorized Transaction List. To edit a memorized transaction, follow these steps:

1. Select Recall Transaction from the Shortcuts pulldown menu or press Ctrl-T to access the Memorized Transaction List.

2. Use the Up and Down Arrow keys to highlight the memorized transaction that you want to edit.

3. Press Ctrl-E to access the Edit/Set Up Memorized Transaction window.

4. Make the necessary changes to the memorized transaction and press F10.

Deleting a Memorized Transaction   To delete a memorized transaction, press Ctrl-T to access the Memorized Transaction List. Then position the arrow on the memorized transaction from the Memorized Transaction List that you want to delete and press Ctrl-D. When Quicken displays the message that you are about to permanently delete a memorized transaction, press Enter.

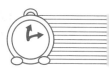

Memorizing Loan Payments

You can memorize loan payments using the loan calculator. Each time you make a payment on a loan, Quicken records the principal and interest amounts from the amortization schedule generated by the loan calculator. Now with Quicken 6, you can amortize fixed rate and variable rate loans and include loan prepayments in the amortization calculation.

Fixed Rate and Variable Rate Loans   The interest rate on a *fixed rate loan* remains constant over the life of the loan. The interest rate on a *variable rate loan,* however, changes in relation to some economic factor, such as the prime lending rate, Treasury Bill interest rates, and so forth.

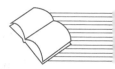

To memorize a loan payment, follow these steps:

1. From the Write Checks screen or the check register, memorize a loan payment transaction as just explained. (Make sure that when you enter the loan payment transaction you enter your mortgage account on the first line of the Split Transaction window and the mortgage interest category on the second line.)

2. Select Recall Transaction from the Shortcuts pull-down menu or press Ctrl-T to access the Memorized Transaction List.

3. Highlight the memorized loan payment and press F9 to select the Amortize option.

4. Quicken displays the Set Amortization Information window as shown in Figure 11.3.

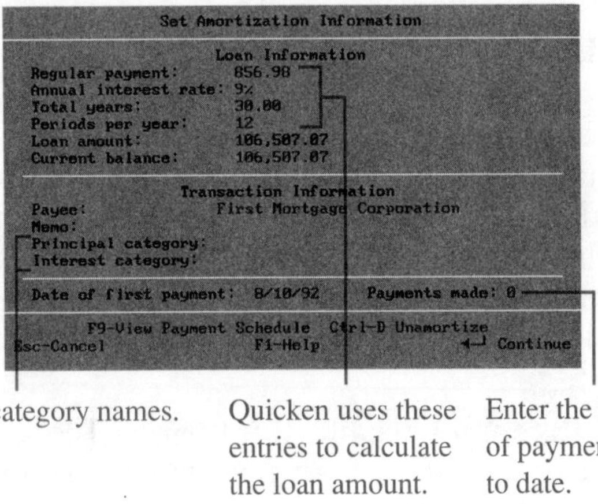

Assign category names.   Quicken uses these   Enter the number
                          entries to calculate of payments made
                          the loan amount.   to date.

Figure 11.3 The Set Amortization Information window to enter loan information.

5. In the Loan Information part of the window, type the payment amount, annual interest rate, loan period (in years), and the number of periods per year. Quicken calculates the approximate loan amount.

6. In the Transaction Information part of the screen, type the payee name, memo (optional), the account to be assigned to the principal portion of the loan payment, and the category name to be assigned to the interest portion of the loan payment.

7. For fixed rate loans, type the date of the first loan payment and the number of payments made to date in the lower part of the window. For variable rate loans, type the date that you will make your next payment and enter zero (0) payments made.

8. Press F9 to view the amortization schedule. Press Ctrl-Enter to amortize the loan payment in the Memorized Transaction List. (Note: Memorized loan payments are designated by an A, for *amortized*, in the Split column of the Memorized Transaction List.)

Recalling Memorized Loan Payments

When you are ready to make a payment on a loan that you have memorized, simply recall the loan payment from the Memorized Transaction List. To recall a memorized loan payment, follow these steps:

1. From an empty line in the register or a blank check in the Write Checks screen, select Recall Transaction from the Shortcuts pull-down menu or press Ctrl-T to access the Memorized Transaction List.

2. Select the loan payment transaction. Quicken displays the Use Amortize Transaction window shown in Figure 11.4.

Figure 11.4 The Use Amortize Transaction window.

3. If the interest rate has changed or you're making a prepayment on the loan, change the appropriate fields in the Use Amortize Transaction window. Press Ctrl-Enter.

4. Quicken records the loan payment and automatically applies the principal and interest amounts to the appropriate account and category.

Canceling a Loan Payment Each time you record a loan payment, Quicken increases the number of payments made on the loan by one. If you mistakenly record a loan payment, you must reset the number of payments made in the Payments Made field in the Set Amortization Information window. After you reset the number of payments, you can delete the recorded payment from the check register.

Last Loan Payment When you recall the last payment on a loan, Quicken reminds you that this is the last payment and will not let you recall this loan payment transaction again.

Printing the List

You may want a hard copy of the transactions that you have memorized. To print the Memorized Transaction List:

1. Select Recall Transaction from the Shortcuts pull-down menu or press Ctrl-T to access the Memorized Transaction List.

2. Press Ctrl-P to select the Print option.

3. Type the number of the printer that you are using if it is different than the default.

4. Press Enter to print the Memorized Transaction List.

In the next lesson, you will learn how to group transactions.

Lesson 12

Grouping Transactions

In this lesson, you will learn how to set up and recall transaction groups.

Setting Up a Transaction Group

A *transaction group* is a group of recurring transactions that you pay or add to your account at the same time.

Transaction groups can have just one transaction or many. Quicken allows you to set up as many as 12 different transaction groups. Examples of transactions that you may want to set up in a transaction group are bills that are due at the beginning of the month, such as your mortgage payment, car loan payment, and insurance payment. To set up a transaction group, follow these steps:

1. Memorize the transactions that you want to include in the transaction group. (See Lesson 11.)

2. From the Write Checks screen or any account register, select Transaction Groups from the Shortcuts pull-down menu or press Ctrl-J to display the Select Transaction Group to Recall window, as in Figure 12.1.

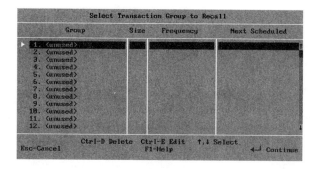

Figure 12.1 Select Transaction Group to Recall window.

3. Use the Up and Down Arrow keys to move the highlight bar to the first <unused> line and press Enter.

4. Quicken displays the Describe Group window, as shown in Figure 12.2.

5. Type a descriptive name for the transaction group, such as Beg of month bills, and press Enter.

6. To automatically load an account before executing the transaction group, type the account name and press Enter. For example, if the transactions are associated with your Quicken checking account, type the account name (as it appears in the Select Account to Use window).

7. If the transaction group has a regular frequency and you want to schedule the group at specific intervals, type the number for the frequency option (see Figure 12.2). Otherwise, leave the frequency set at 1. Press Enter.

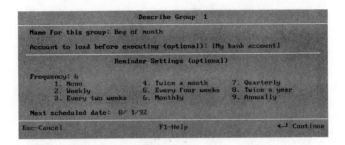

Figure 12.2 Describe Group window.

8. If you want to be reminded that the transactions in the transaction group are due, type the date that you first want to be reminded of the transaction group due date. (Note: When a transaction group is due, Quicken will only remind you of the due date. Quicken will not recall the transaction group automatically.)

9. Press Ctrl-Enter to record the information.

10. Quicken next displays the Assign Transactions to Group window (Figure 12.3). (Note: The transactions included in the Assign Transactions to Group window are transactions that you have previously memorized.)

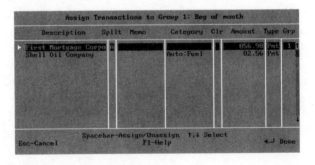

Figure 12.3 Assign Transactions to Group window.

11. Use the arrow keys to highlight each transaction to include in the transaction group.

12. Press the Spacebar to assign the highlighted transaction to the transaction group. The group number appears in the Grp column next to each transaction included in the transaction group. (Note: You can assign a transaction to more than one group.)

13. When you are finished assigning transactions, press Enter to set up the transaction group.

Transaction Groups for Printing Checks   To set up a transaction group for printing checks, be sure that you memorize transactions (for the transaction group) at the Write Checks screen. Transactions assigned at the Write Checks screen have the word Chk in the Type column of the Assign Transactions to Group window.

Adding a Transaction to a Transaction Group

You can add transactions to a transaction group at any time. To add a transaction to a transaction group:

1. From the Write Checks screen or any account register, select Transaction Groups from the Shortcuts pull-down menu or press Ctrl-J to display the Select Transaction Group to Execute window.

2. Use the arrow keys to highlight the transaction group to which you want to add a transaction.

3. Press Ctrl-E to access the Describe Group window.

4. Press Ctrl-Enter to show the list of memorized transactions.

5. Use the arrow keys to highlight the transaction you want to add to the transaction group.

6. Press the Spacebar to assign the highlighted transaction and press Enter to add the transaction.

Editing a Transaction Group

You can change the description or the assigned transactions in a transaction group at any time. To edit a transaction group, follow these steps:

1. From the Write Checks screen or any account register, select Transaction Groups from the Shortcuts pulldown menu or press Ctrl-J to display the Select Transaction Group to Execute window.

2. Use the arrow keys to highlight the transaction group that you want to edit.

3. Press Ctrl-E to access the Describe Group window.

4. To edit any of the information in the Describe Group window, make the changes and press Ctrl-Enter.

5. Quicken displays the Assign Transactions to Group window. To assign or unassign a transaction, use the Up and Down Arrow keys to highlight the transaction, then press the Spacebar.

6. Press Enter to save the changes to the transaction group.

Deleting a Transaction Group   Press Ctrl-J to display the Select Transaction Group to Execute window and use the arrow keys to highlight the transaction group that you want to delete. Then press Ctrl-D and Enter to delete the transaction group.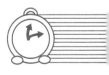

Recalling a Transaction Group

To record the transactions in a transaction group in the account register, you must recall the transaction group. When you do so, Quicken enters each transaction in the account register or the Write Checks screen. You can then make changes, if necessary, to transactions. To recall a transaction group:

1. From the Write Checks screen or any account register, select Transaction Groups from the Shortcuts pull-down menu or press Ctrl-J to display the Select Transaction Group to Execute window.

2. Use the arrow keys to highlight the transaction group you want to recall and press Enter.

3. Quicken displays the Transaction Group Date window, showing the date that will be given to the transactions.

4. Use the + or – keys to change the date if needed and press Enter. (Note: If you are recalling a transaction group with a memorized loan payment, Quicken displays the Use Amortize Transaction window. See Lesson 11.)

5. Quicken displays a message that the transactions from the group have been entered in the account register.

6. Press Enter.

 **Checks to be Printed** If the transactions in the recalled transaction group include checks that you want to print at this time, press Ctrl-W to display the Write Checks screen and then press Ctrl-P to print the checks.

In the next lesson, you learn how to reconcile your bank account.

Lesson 13

Reconciling Your Bank Account

In this lesson, you will learn how to reconcile your bank account to your Quicken check register.

A bank reconciliation is a procedure to compare the balance shown on your bank statement at the end of a specific period to the balance shown in the check register at the end of the same period. You should reconcile your account with your bank statement each time you receive a statement to ensure that:

- You successfully recorded the same transactions that the bank statement shows.

- Your recorded transactions are accurate.

- The bank statement correctly reflects your transactions for the period. (Banks sometimes make mistakes!)

Entering Information from Your Bank Statement

You must enter the information shown on your bank statement in Quicken before you can reconcile your bank account. To enter information from your bank statement:

1. Press Ctrl-R from the Main menu to access the check register. Make sure that the register you access is the register for the bank account you are reconciling.

2. Select Reconcile from the Activities pull-down menu.

3. Quicken displays the Reconcile Register with Bank Statement window shown in Figure 13.1. (Note: The first time that you use Quicken to reconcile, Quicken displays an introductory message. Press F10 to continue). Compare the opening balance shown in the window with the opening balance shown on your statement. If this is the first time you have reconciled your account, there may be a difference in the Bank Statement Opening Balance field. If necessary, type the correct opening balance and press Enter.

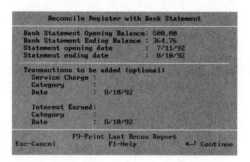

Figure 13.1   The Reconcile Register with Bank Statement window.

4. Type the ending balance on your bank statement and press Enter.

5. Type any transactions to be added (service charges and interest earned) and a category name to allocate the transactions, if desired. (Note: If you want to see your last reconciliation report, press F9 from the Reconcile Register with Bank Statement window to print a copy.)

6. Press Ctrl-Enter to record the information in the Reconcile Register with Bank Statement window.

7. Quicken next displays a list of uncleared transactions and a Reconciliation Summary.

Marking Cleared Transactions

The next step in reconciling your bank account is to mark all of the cleared transactions in the check register.

Cleared Transactions *Cleared transactions* are transactions that are recorded in the check register and *have been* processed by the bank. Cleared transactions may include deposits, checks (withdrawals), ATM transactions, and so on.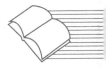

To mark cleared transactions, follow these steps:

1. From the list of uncleared transactions (see Figure 13.2) which is displayed after information is entered in the Reconcile Register with Bank Statement window, use the Up and Down Arrow keys to highlight each transaction that appears on your bank statement.

Check number column   Clear column

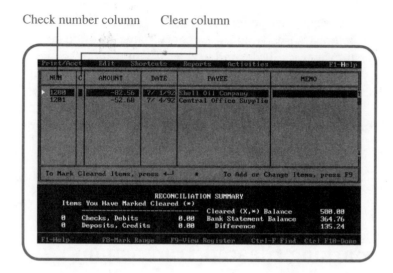

Figure 13.2   Marking cleared transactions.

2. For each transaction highlighted, press Enter to mark
the transaction as cleared. Quicken will enter an asterisk in the Clear column (the column next to the Check
Number column) to show that the transaction has cleared.
To unmark a transaction, highlight the transaction and
press the Spacebar.

   Marking a Range of Cleared Checks   If an un-
   interrupted sequence of checks appears on your
   bank statement as cleared, you can mark the range
   as cleared without marking each individual check.
   Press F8 to display the Mark Range of Check
   Numbers as Cleared window. Then type the beginning and ending check numbers for the range of
   checks that you want to mark as cleared and press
   Enter.

Completing the Bank Reconciliation

The reconciliation can be completed after you have marked all cleared transactions. To complete the bank reconciliation, follow these steps:

1. Review the RECONCILIATION SUMMARY at the bottom of the uncleared transactions list. If the difference is zero, then your bank account balances, and you may complete the reconciliation. If the difference is a value other than zero(see the next section), then you need to either find the difference or have Quicken adjust your check register balance to agree with the bank statement balance.

2. If your bank account balances, then press Ctrl-F10 from the uncleared transactions list to have Quicken reconcile your account.

3. Quicken displays a congratulatory message and asks if you want to print a Reconciliation Report.

4. If you want to print the report, type Y and then press Enter. (Note: You do not have to print the Reconciliation Report to complete the bank reconciliation.)

5. Quicken displays the Print Reconciliation Report window. Type the number of the printer to send the report to and press Enter.

6. Type a reconcile date if you want the date on the report to be a date other than the current date. Press Enter.

7. If you want a detailed report, change the S to F and press Enter.

8. Type a report title, if desired.

9. Press Ctrl-Enter to print the report.

Adjusting for Differences

If the difference shown in the Reconciliation Summary is a value other than zero, then you can go back through the transactions to try to locate the difference, or have Quicken make an adjustment in your check register for the difference. To have Quicken adjust the difference:

1. Press Ctrl-F10 from the uncleared transactions list to have Quicken reconcile your account.

2. If the difference is due to a discrepancy between the opening balance in your account and the opening balance on your statement, Quicken asks if you want to create a balance adjustment. Press Y to create the adjustment or N to complete the reconciliation without adjusting the register balance.

3. If the difference results from the transactions during the period, Quicken displays the Problem: Check Register does not balance with Bank Statement window. Press Enter to continue and Quicken next displays the Adding Balance Adjustment Entry window.

4. Quicken tells you what the adjusting entry will be and asks if you want to add it to the register. Press Y to add the adjustment to the register and type a category name (optional) for this transaction.

5. Press Ctrl-Enter to create the adjusting entry.

Deleting Adjusting Entries   Adjusting entries can be deleted from the check register if you later find the error that resulted in the reconciliation difference.

In the next lesson, you will learn how to set up and use a credit card account.

Lesson 14

Working with Credit Card Accounts

In this lesson, you will learn how to set up a credit card account that you can use to track your credit card transactions. You'll also learn how to use IntelliCharge.

If you pay your credit card bills on a current basis (pay the balance each month), you probably do not need to set up a credit card account. You can enter credit card transactions in the check register when you pay your credit card bill and split the transaction so that you can assign a separate category to each transaction. However, if you do not pay your credit card bill on a current basis, you should set up a credit card account to track your credit card purchases and payments.

Credit Card Account   A *credit card account* is a Quicken account used to enter credit card purchases and payments. A separate account should be set up for each of your credit card accounts. You can set up a credit card account for MasterCard, Visa, Discover, etc.

If you have a Quicken Visa card and want to receive your statements on disk or by modem, you must set up a credit card account and designate the account as an IntelliCharge account.

IntelliCharge *IntelliCharge* is a new service that updates your credit card register automatically by disk or modem. When you use IntelliCharge, you avoid entering credit transactions in your credit card register; IntelliCharge does that for you.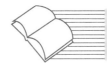

Setting Up a Credit Card Account

To set up a credit card account, refer to Lesson 3 for an explanation on setting up a new account. Go to the Set Up New Account window (shown in Figure 3.2) and follow these steps:

1. Press 2 to select Credit Card in the Account Type field in the Set Up New Account window. Press Enter.

2. Type the name of the credit card account and press Enter.

3. Quicken displays the Starting Balance and Description window shown in Figure 14.1.

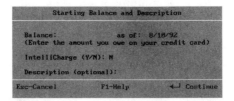

Figure 14.1 The Starting Balance and Description window.

4. Type the starting balance in the credit card account and press Enter. This is the account balance as of the date that you specify (in the next step) as the start date.

5. Type the date that relates to the starting balance you entered in step 4 and press Enter. If you are using your last credit card statement balance, enter the statement date.

6. If you want to designate this credit card account as an IntelliCharge account, press Y in the IntelliCharge field.

7. For regular credit card accounts, type a description (optional) of the account and press Enter. It is useful to enter the credit card account number here. Go to step 9.

For IntelliCharge accounts, type the account number and press Enter. Go to the next step.

8. For IntelliCharge accounts, Quicken displays the IntelliCharge Account Information window shown in Figure 14.2. Press Y if you would like to receive your statement by modem, otherwise, leave the setting at N to receive your statement on disk. Next, type your social security number and press Ctrl-Enter.

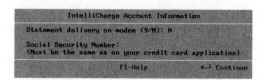

Figure 14.2 The IntelliCharge Account Information window.

If you choose to receive your statement by modem, Quicken displays the IntelliCharge Phone Number and Password window. Enter the local phone number for the CompuServe network where your statements will be downloaded. Type a password next to prevent unauthorized access to your statement file. Passwords can be up to 8 characters in length, but must be at least 4 non-blank characters. Press Enter.

9. Quicken displays the Specify Credit Limit window. Type the credit limit that applies to this credit card account (optional).

10. Press Enter to add the credit card account or the IntelliCharge account to the Quicken account list.

Entering Transactions in the Credit Card Register

For regular credit card accounts, enter credit card purchases and finance charges in the credit card register throughout the month as you make purchases, or at the end of the month when you receive your monthly statement. To enter transactions in the credit card register, follow these steps:

1. Choose Select Account from the Main menu to display the Select Account to Use window or, from the Write Checks screen or any register, press Ctrl-A.

2. Use the Up and Down Arrow keys to highlight the credit card account that you want to use and press Enter.

3. Quicken displays the credit card register (see Figure 14.3) for the account that you selected. (Note: The credit card register resembles the check register.)

Amount charged —— Amount paid

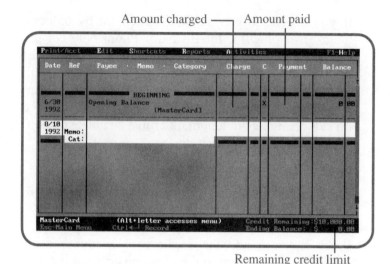

Remaining credit limit
after charges are recorded.

Figure 14.3 The credit card register.

4. Enter transactions the same way you do in the check register. (Refer to Lesson 5.)

Entering Transactions You can memorize and recall transactions in the credit card register. (Refer to Lesson 11.) You can also split transactions in the credit card register. (Refer to Lesson 10.)

Marking Cleared Credit Card Transactions If you enter credit card purchases from your monthly statement, type an asterisk (*) in the C (Clear) column when you enter the transaction. This will save you time when you reconcile your credit card account.

Updating IntelliCharge Accounts

Updating your IntelliCharge credit card account is the same as entering credit card transactions in a regular credit card account, except that IntelliCharge enters the transactions automatically for you, either from a disk file or by modem.

To receive your statement on disk or by modem, follow these steps:

1. Access the register for your IntelliCharge credit card account.

2. Select Get IntelliCharge Data from the Activities pull-down menu.

3. Quicken displays the Get IntelliCharge Data window. If you're receiving your statement on disk, type the disk drive your statement disk is in and press Enter. If you're receiving your statement by modem, turn on your modem and press Enter.

4. Quicken displays the Updating Account window with each of your credit card transactions. After all credit card transactions are read from the disk file or the downloaded file, Quicken displays the IntelliCharge Statement window that shows the date, payee, amount, and category for each credit card transaction.

5. Press Ctrl-Enter to record the transactions in the credit card register. Quicken displays the Make Credit Card Payment window. The steps to make payment on an IntelliCharge account are the same as steps 9 through 12 in the next section. Follow the steps in the next section.

Reconciling and Paying Your Credit Card Account

Quicken reconciles your credit card account and creates a transaction for any expenses that are shown on your credit card statement but are not reflected in the credit card register, such as finance charges or credit card fees. Quicken then gives you the option of paying the credit card company through a handwritten check or a Quicken check. (Note: The first eight steps in this section are not necessary for IntelliCharge accounts.)

To reconcile and pay your credit card account, follow these steps:

1. From the credit card register, select the Reconcile/Pay Credit Card option from the Activities pull-down menu.

2. Quicken displays the Credit Card Statement Information window as shown in Figure 14.4.

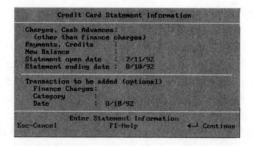

Figure 14.4 The Credit Card Statement Information window for entering information from your monthly statement.

3. Type charges, cash advances, payments, credits, the new balance, and the opening and ending dates from your credit card statement and press Enter.

4. Type finance charges (optional) and a category name to allocate finance charges.

5. Press Ctrl-Enter to display the uncleared transactions list.

6. Use the Up and Down Arrow keys to highlight each transaction that appears on your credit card statement. For each transaction highlighted, press Enter to mark the transaction as cleared. Quicken will enter an asterisk in the column next to the Reference column to show that the transaction has cleared. (Note: In the last lesson you learned how to mark a range of transactions as cleared. You can also mark ranges of transactions in the credit card register.)

Switching to the Credit Card Register If you need to go back to the credit card register while you are marking transactions in the uncleared transactions list, press F9. Press F9 again to go back to the uncleared transactions list.

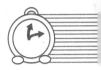

7. Press Ctrl-F10 when you are finished marking cleared transactions.

8. Review the Reconciliation Summary at the bottom of the uncleared transactions list. If the difference is zero, then your credit card account balances, and you may go on to step 9 and complete the reconciliation. If the difference is a value other than zero, then you need to either find the difference (press Esc) or have Quicken adjust your credit card register balance to agree with your credit card statement (press Enter at the Adjusting Register to Agree with Statement window).

9. If your credit card account balances, Quicken displays the Make Credit Card Payment window.

10. Type the name of the checking account (or press Ctrl-C for a listing of accounts) to use to pay the credit card bill and press Enter.

11. Press N to make out a Quicken check, or Y to make out a handwritten check.

12. Press Enter to process and record the payment in the check register and in the credit card register, or press Esc if you do not want to pay the credit card bill now.

Transferring Funds to Your Credit Card Account

When you pay your credit card bill, you can automatically transfer funds from your bank account to your credit card account. Note: If you write a Quicken check to pay your credit card bill (as explained in the previous section), the following steps are carried out automatically.

To transfer funds to your credit card account, follow these steps:

1. From the Write Checks screen or the check register, enter the payment to the credit card company.

2. In the Category field, type the name of the credit card account to which you want the funds (or payment) transferred. Quicken enters the name of the credit card account enclosed in brackets to indicate a transfer.

3. Press Ctrl-Enter to record the payment.

4. Quicken enters the payment amount as a PAYMENT to your credit card account and decreases the outstanding balance by the amount of the payment.

Transferring Funds from Your Credit Card Account

If your credit card account provides for cash advances or overdraft protection for your bank account, you can transfer funds from your credit card account to your bank account. To transfer funds from your credit card account, follow these steps:

1. From the credit card register, enter the charge to your credit card account.

2. In the Category field, type the name of the bank account to which you want the funds transferred. Quicken enters the name of the bank account enclosed in brackets to indicate a transfer.

3. Press Ctrl-Enter to record the charge.

4. Quicken enters the charge amount as a DEPOSIT to your bank account and increases the outstanding balance by the amount of the charge.

   In the next lesson, you will learn how to set up and use a cash account.

Lesson 15

Working with Cash Accounts

In this lesson, you will learn how to set up a cash account that you can use to keep track of your cash expenditures.

A *cash account* is a Quicken account used to track cash transactions. Cash accounts should be used if you prefer to use cash instead of checks or credit cards, if you normally get paid in cash, or in the case of a business, if you must track petty cash.

Setting Up a Cash Account

To set up a cash account, refer to Lesson 3 for an explanation on setting up a new account. Go to the Set Up New Account window (shown in Figure 3.2) and follow these steps:

1. Press 3 to select Cash Account in the Account Type field in the Set Up New Account window and press Enter.

2. Type the name of the cash account and press Enter.

3. Quicken displays the Starting Balance and Description window.

4. Type the starting balance in the cash account and press Enter. This is the amount of cash on hand as of the date that you specify (in the next step) as the start date.

5. Type the date that relates to the starting balance entered in step 4 and press Enter.

6. Type a description (optional) of the account.

7. Press Ctrl-Enter to add the cash account to the Quicken account list.

Entering Cash Transactions in the Cash Register

To enter cash transactions in the cash register, follow these steps:

1. Choose Select Account from the Main menu to display the Select Account to Use window.

2. Use the Up and Down Arrow keys to highlight the cash account and press Enter.

3. Quicken displays the cash register shown in Figure 15.1. (Note: The cash register resembles the check register.)

4. Enter transactions the same way as they are entered in the check register (see Lesson 5).

Entering Cash Transactions You can memo-rize and recall transactions in the cash register (see Lesson 11). You can also split transactions in the cash register (see Lesson 10).

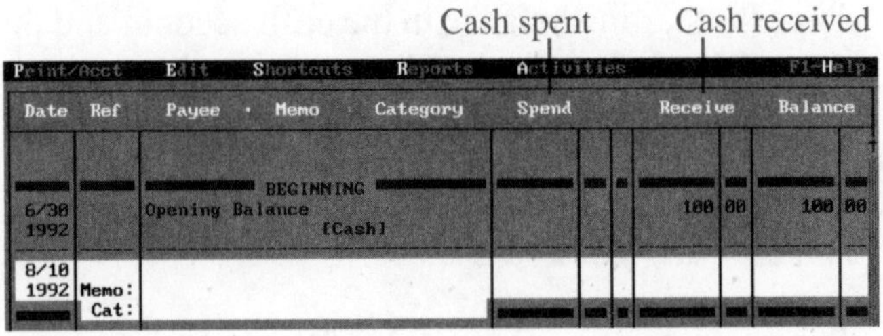

Cash spent   Cash received

Figure 15.1   The cash register.

Transferring Funds to Your Cash Account

With just one transaction, funds can be transferred from your Quicken bank account to your cash account. To transfer funds to your cash account, follow these steps:

1. From the Write Checks screen or the check register, enter the transaction for the withdrawal.

2. In the Category field, type the name of the cash account to which you want the funds transferred. Quicken enters the name of the cash account enclosed in brackets to indicate a transfer.

3. Press Ctrl-Enter to record the transfer.

4. Quicken records the cash amount as a RECEIVE entry in the cash account and increases the cash balance by the amount of the transfer.

Updating Your Cash Account Balance

Reconciliations are performed on bank accounts and credit card accounts. Although it is not necessary to perform a reconciliation on a cash account, you should periodically update your cash account balance to accurately reflect your cash on hand. To update your cash account balance, follow these steps:

1. From the cash register, select Update Account Balance from the Activities pull-down menu.

2. Quicken displays the Update Account Balance window shown in Figure 15.2.

Cash on hand

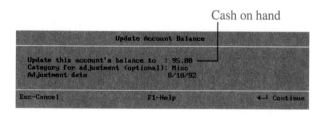

Figure 15.2   The Update Account Balance window.

3. Type the amount of cash on hand and press Enter.

4. Type the category name (optional) for this adjusting transaction.

5. Press Enter to update your cash account balance. If the amount of cash that you entered is more than the cash account balance, Quicken enters an adjustment in the

109

RECEIVE column of the cash register. If the amount of cash that you entered is less than the cash account balance, Quicken enters an adjustment in the SPEND column of the cash register.

In the next lesson, you will learn how to use Quicken's loan calculator.

Lesson 16

Using the Loan Calculator

In this lesson, you will learn how to use Quicken's on-screen loan calculator to amortize loans.

Accessing the Loan Calculator

Quicken enables you to amortize loans with its on-screen loan calculator. With the loan calculator, you can perform "what if" calculations to determine the effect of changes in interest rates, principal amounts, and payment periods. Now with Quicken 6, you can choose the type of calculation you want to perform with the loan calculator. The calculator is no longer limited to just calculating a loan payment. You can also calculate the principal or original amount of a loan.

To access the loan calculator, follow these steps:

1. From the Write Checks screen or any register screen, press Alt-A to access the Activities pull-down menu.

2. Press F to select Financial Planning.

3. Quicken displays the Financial Planning menu.

4. Select the Loan Calculator to display the Quicken loan calculator as shown in Figure 16.1.

The checkmark indicates the calculation Quicken performs. —————

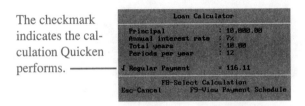

Figure 16.1 The loan calculator.

Using the Loan Calculator

To amortize loans using the loan calculator, follow these steps:

1. Access the loan calculator as just explained.

2. Press F8 to select the calculation you want to make. Quicken shows a check mark next to the field it will calculate (Principal or Regular Payment).

3. Type the principal amount of the loan (if calculating the regular payment), the annual interest rate (up to four decimal places), the total years (period of time that the loan covers), the number of periods (payments) per year, and the payment amount (if calculating the principal of a loan).

4. After you enter the information in the loan calculator, Quicken calculates the payment amount and displays it in the Regular Payment field, or calculates the principal or original amount of the loan and displays it in the Principal field.

5. Press Esc to clear the loan calculator from the screen.

Viewing the Payment Schedule

After you calculate the loan payment or the principal amount of a loan using the loan calculator, you can view the payment schedule. The payment schedule lists the payment number, interest and principal allocated to each payment, and the remaining principal balance. To view the payment schedule, follow these steps:

1. Calculate the regular payment amount or the principal amount using the loan calculator as just explained.

2. Press F9 to display the Approximate Payment Schedule window shown in Figure 16.2. You can move up and down the window to view the entire payment schedule.

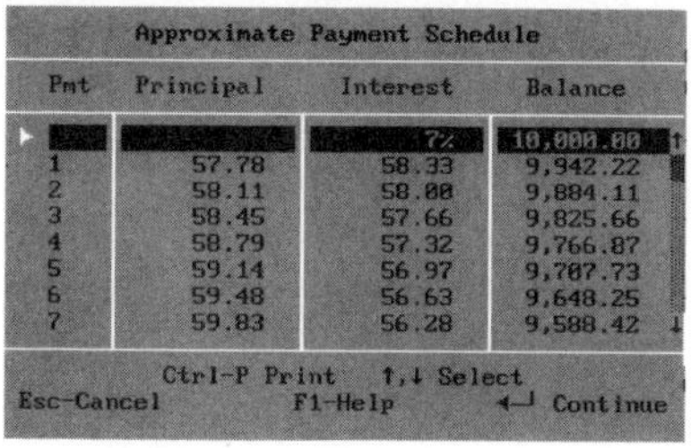

Pmt	Principal	Interest	Balance
		7%	10,000.00
1	57.78	58.33	9,942.22
2	58.11	58.00	9,884.11
3	58.45	57.66	9,825.66
4	58.79	57.32	9,766.87
5	59.14	56.97	9,707.73
6	59.48	56.63	9,648.25
7	59.83	56.28	9,588.42

Ctrl-P Print ↑,↓ Select
Esc-Cancel   F1-Help   ← Continue

Figure 16.2 The Approximate Payment Schedule window.

Printing the Payment Schedule

To print the Loan Payment schedule, follow these steps:

1. Display the Approximate Payment Schedule window for a loan as just explained.

113

2. Press Ctrl-P to print the Loan Payment schedule and type the number of the printer that you are using.

In the next lesson, you learn how to create and print reports.

Lesson 17
Creating and Printing Reports

In this lesson, you will learn how to create and print Quicken's standard reports.

The Quicken program includes preset reports that can be viewed on your screen or printed. Preset reports consist of 7 personal reports, 8 business reports, and 5 investment reports. In addition, Quicken allows you to create your own custom reports or customize any of the preset reports. Quicken 6 includes the Redo Last Report option (Ctrl-Z), which redisplays the last report that you created.

Creating Reports

To create reports, follow these steps:

1. Select Create Reports from the Main menu or press Alt-R from any register or the Write Checks screen. Quicken displays the Reports menu.

2. Select one of the following options:

    Personal Reports

Business Reports

Investment Reports

3. A different list of reports is displayed, dependent on your selection in step 2. For example, if you selected Personal Reports, Quicken displays a list of seven reports that you can create for your personal needs (see Figure 17.1).

Figure 17.1   The list of personal reports.

4. Select the report that you want to create to display the report window. Figure 17.2 shows the Cash Flow Report window.

5. Type a report title (optional) and the date(s) that the report is to cover. (Note: The report window for investment reports requires additional information such as how to subtotal the report and whether to include current, all, or selected investment accounts in the report.) When you have finished filling in the report window, press Ctrl-Enter to create the report. Quicken searches through the transactions and displays the report on your screen.

Printing Reports

Reports that you have created can be printed. However, before printing reports, you must assign printer settings in Quicken.

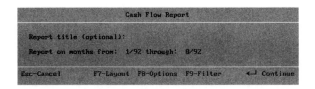

Figure 17.2 The Cash Flow Report window.

To assign printer settings in Quicken, refer to Lesson 9. To assign printer settings for reports, use the same procedure but select Report Printer Settings from the Printer Settings menu.

To print reports, follow these steps:

1. Position paper in your printer and turn it on.

2. With the report displayed on your screen, select Print Report from the File/Print pull-down menu or simply press Ctrl-P.

3. Quicken displays the Print Report window shown in Figure 17.3.

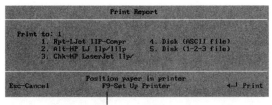

Press F9 to specify printer settings if you haven't already done so.

Figure 17.3 The Print Report window for printing a report.

4. Type the number of the printer to which you want to send the report. Press 1 for the report printer that you set

up. If you want the report sent to the alternate report printer, press 2.

5. Press Enter to send the report to your printer.

Changing Printer Settings   If you need to change the printer settings that are shown in the Print Report window, press F9 from the Print Report window. Quicken allows you to change the printer settings while the report is still on your screen.

In the next lesson, you learn how to use other report features in Quicken.

Lesson 18

Using Other Report Features

In this lesson, you will learn how to further customize your Quicken reports.

Moving Around the Report Screen

When a report is on-screen, you may need to move around the report screen to examine the detail behind a report entry or to view another entry. To move around the report:

Press	To Move
Tab or Right Arrow	One column to the right.
Shift-Tab or Left Arrow	One column to the left.
Ctrl-Right Arrow	One screen to the right.
Ctrl-Left Arrow	One screen to the left.
PgUp and PgDn	Up or down one screen.
Home	To the far left, current row.
End	To the far right, current row.
Home-Home	To the top left corner of the report.
End-End	To the bottom right corner of the report.

Editing Reports in the Report Screen

You can edit reports while they are on your screen through the use of pull-down menus. With the report on-screen, you can do the following:

- Print and memorize reports

- Examine (QuickZoom) report detail

- Set titles and date ranges

- Filter transactions, accounts, categories, and classes

- Change the layout of the report

- Collapse or expand report detail

Note that some of the above features are beyond the scope of this book.

Using QuickZoom

QuickZoom allows you to examine the transaction detail behind a report entry. (Note: This feature can only be used with noninvestment transaction, summary, and budget reports.) To use QuickZoom, follow these steps:

1. With the report displayed on your screen, move the cursor to the report entry that you want to examine.

2. Select QuickZoom from the File/Print pull-down menu or just press Ctrl-Z. If you are using a mouse, double-click on the report entry.

3. For summary or budget reports, Quicken displays a Transaction List window (Figure 18.1). For transaction reports, it displays the register entry for the report entry.

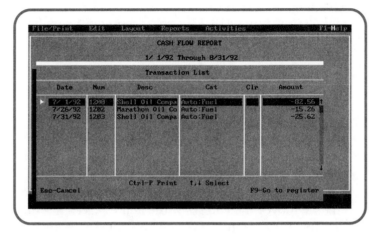

Figure 18.1 The Transaction List window listing the transaction detail behind a report entry.

4. To display the register entry for a transaction listed in the Transaction List window, move the cursor to the transaction and press F9.

5. To return to the report screen, press Ctrl-Z.

Using the Collapse Feature

The collapse feature allows you to summarize the detail for a row heading in summary, budget, or account balance reports without changing the report totals. For example, if you want to present Total Inflows in a Cash Flow Report as just one line in the report, you can collapse the row heading and Quicken reduces the Total Inflows section of the report to a single line. (Note: You cannot use the collapse feature with transaction reports.) To collapse a row heading:

1. With the report displayed on your screen, position the cursor on the row heading that you want to summarize or collapse. Figure 18.2 shows a report before collapsing a row heading.

2. Select Collapse from the Layout pull-down menu, press – (minus), or double-click on the row heading.

3. Quicken now displays one line for the row heading, as shown in Figure 18.3.

When you collapse a category within a section of a report, Quicken moves the category to the end of the section and then removes the *category* title and replaces it with a *hidden* title. For example, if you collapse the Salary Income category in the Inflows section of a cash flow report, Quicken moves the category to the end of the Inflows section and replaces the Salary Income title with the title Inflows—Hidden.

Expanding Report Detail

Return any detail in a report that is summarized or collapsed to its original format with the Expand feature. To expand report detail:

1. Place the cursor on the row heading you want to expand.

2. Select Expand from the Layout pull-down menu, press +, or double-click on the row heading.

3. Quicken displays the detail for the row heading.

Heading selected before collapse

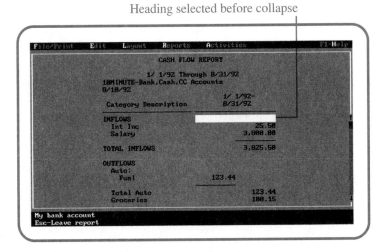

Figure 18.2   A sample report that shows a row heading before it has been collapsed.

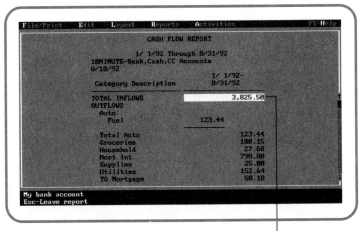

Collapsed information appears in one line.

Figure 18.3   A sample report that shows a row heading after it has been collapsed.

Setting Report Options Setting report options allows you to choose how the report is organized, how transfers are handled, and how dollars and cents and subcategories are displayed. For transaction reports, you can choose how totals, split transactions, memos, and categories are displayed. To set report options, press F8 from the report window to display the Report Options window. Fill in the Report Options window and press Ctrl-Enter to return to the report window. If you want to reset the report options, press Ctrl-D at the Report Options window.

Changing Report Layout Once you have created and displayed a report on-screen, you can change the report layout using the options on the Layout pull-down menu (Alt-L).

Memorizing Reports

You can memorize regularly used reports so that you can access them quickly. To memorize reports:

1. From the report screen, press Ctrl-M to display the Memorize Report window.

2. Type a report title, if desired. Press Enter.

Accessing Memorized Reports

To access a memorized report, follow these steps:

1. Select Memorized Reports from the Reports menu. Quicken displays the Memorized Reports List.

2. Use the Up and Down arrow keys to highlight the report that you want to access and press Enter. Note that from the Memorized Reports List you can edit a memorized report (press Ctrl-E to edit) and delete a memorized report (press Ctrl-D to delete).

   In the next lesson, you will learn how to set up a budget in Quicken.

Lesson 19

Budgeting with Quicken

In this lesson, you will learn how to set up budget amounts for the categories that you use in Quicken.

Budgeting is a procedure for allocating income and expenses on a monthly basis and comparing those allocated amounts to actual amounts. For example, if you normally spend $50 per month for auto repairs, then you would allocate, or budget, $50 to a category for auto repairs and assign that category to all transactions relating to auto repairs. At the end of any given month, you can compare the actual amount spent on auto repairs to the budgeted, or allocated amount for auto repairs.

To use Quicken's budget capabilities, you must set up categories and assign transactions to categories. If you haven't been working with categories, you can set up categories now and either start assigning categories henceforth, or go back to prior transactions in the check register and assign categories.

Assigning Categories To ensure that all transactions are assigned to categories, you can set one of the Quicken transaction settings to display an assign category message each time you record a transaction. To select this setting, press Y at the

`Warn if transaction has no category` line from the
Transaction Settings menu. (See Lesson 2 for more
on the Transactions Settings menu.)

Entering Budget Amounts

Budget amounts are entered for monthly periods only. You
can enter monthly budget amounts and convert them to
quarterly or yearly amounts (this feature is covered later in
this lesson). Budget amounts can be changed at any time.
To enter budget amounts:

1. From the Write Checks screen or any noninvestment
   register, select Set Up Budgets from the Activities pull-
   down menu. Quicken displays the budgeting spreadsheet shown in Figure 19.1. The budgeting spreadsheet
   displays categories on the far left side of the screen and
   monthly columns to enter budget amounts by category.
   (Note: Subcategories and accounts are also displayed if
   the Budget Subcats and Budget Transfers options are
   selected. These options are explained later in this lesson.) Categories in the budgeting spreadsheet are di-
   vided into two parts: *inflows* and *outflows*. Quicken
   compares total inflows to total outflows and displays
   the difference.

2. Move through the monthly columns. Type a budget
   amount (and press Enter) for some or all categories.

3. Press Esc to leave the budgeting spreadsheet and return
   to the screen you were previously working in. (Budget
   amounts are automatically saved.)

Printing Budgets Select **P**rint Budgets from the **F**ile pull-down menu, or just press Ctrl-P, to print a copy of the budget amounts set up in the budgeting spreadsheet. Actual amounts will not be printed. (See Creating Budgeting Reports later in this lesson.)

Categories and Subcategories   Monthly budgeting columns

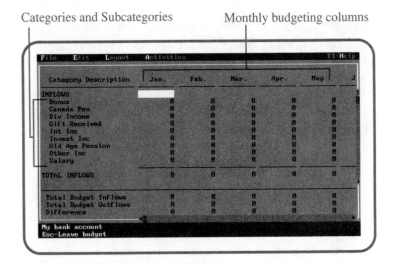

Figure 19.1 The Quicken budgeting spreadsheet for entering budget amounts.

Budgeting Subcategories and Transfers

When you access the Budgeting screen, subcategories and transfers (accounts) are not displayed. To set up budget amounts for subcategories and transfers, you must tell Quicken to display them on the Budgeting screen. To budget subcategories and transfers:

1. From the Write Checks screen or any noninvestment register, select Set Up Budgets from the Activities pull-down menu. Quicken displays the budgeting spreadsheet shown in Figure 19.1.

2. From the Edit pull-down menu, select the Budget Subcats or the Budget Transfers option.

3. Quicken then displays all subcategories or accounts (if you chose to budget transfers).

4. Enter amounts for subcategories and transfers.

To quickly move through the Budgeting screen to enter budget amounts, use the keys explained in Table 19.1.

Table 19.1 Moving within the budgeting spreadsheet.

Keys	Function
Ctrl-Left/Right arrow	To move left or right one column.
Tab	Move from month to month in the same row.
Shift-Tab	Move back one month.
Quote (") or Apostrophe Keys (')	Copies the amount from the previous month to the current month.
Home	Moves to the beginning of an entry field or to the first column in a row of calculated fields.
Home-Home	Moves to the first column in a row of entry fields or to the upper left corner of the screen from a calculated field.
Home-Home-Home	Moves to the upper left corner of the screen from an entry field.

continues

129

Table 19.1   Continued

Keys	Function
End	Moves to the end of an entry field or to the last column in a row of calculated fields.
End-End	Moves to the last column in a row of entry fields or to the lower right corner of the screen from a calculated field.
End-End-End	Moves to the lower right corner of the screen from an entry field.

Clearing the Budgeting Spreadsheet   To remove all budget data from the budgeting spreadsheet, select the Clear Budget option from the Edit pull-down menu.

Setting Up Budget Amounts from Actual Data

If you want to set up your budget amounts using actual amounts from your account registers, Quicken provides the AutoCreate option that automatically fills the columns in the Budgeting screen with the actual income, expense, and transfer amounts for any time period in the current Quicken file. To set up budget amounts from actual data:

1. From the budgeting spreadsheet, select the AutoCreate option from the Edit pull-down menu.

2. Quicken displays the Automatically Create Budget window shown in Figure 19.2.

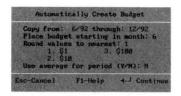

Figure 19.2   The Automatically Create Budget window.

3. In the Copy from field, type the time period that you want actual data extracted from. Then type the number of the first month in the budgeting spreadsheet that you want actual data recorded in. For example, if you want actual data from a three month period recorded in June, July, and August in the budgeting spreadsheet, you would enter 6, since June is the 6th month of the year. (Note: The number of months of actual data must equal the number of months to be recorded in the budgeting spreadsheet.)

4. Next, specify how actual amounts should be rounded.

5. Lastly, press Y if you want Quicken to compute income, expense, and transfer averages for any number of months and enter the average amounts in any month in the budgeting spreadsheet.

6. Press F10 to set up budget amounts.

Copying Budget Amounts to Other Months

If your budget amounts are the same from month to month, you can use the Fill Right or Fill Columns options to copy budget amounts from one month to other months. To copy budget amounts to other months, follow these steps:

1. From the Write Checks screen or any noninvestment register, select Set Up Budgets from the Activities pull-down menu. Quicken displays the budgeting spreadsheet shown in Figure 19.1.

2. From the Edit pull-down menu, select one of the following options:

   Fill Right—copies the highlighted budget amount to each month to the right in the *current* row.

   Fill **C**olumns—copies the highlighted budget amount column to all months to the right in *every* row.

3. Quicken automatically fills in each row/column.

Setting Up Budget Amounts that Occur Every Two Weeks

If you have budget amounts that occur every two weeks, instead of every month, you can use the Two Week option to set up those budget amounts. To set up budget amounts that occur every two weeks, follow these steps:

1. At the budgeting spreadsheet, position the highlight bar in the category row that you want to budget on two-week intervals.

2. From the Edit pull-down menu, select the Two Week option. Quicken displays the Set Up 2 Week Budget window.

3. Enter the amount you want to budget. Press Enter.

4. Enter the starting date for the two-week interval.

5. Press F10 to set up two-week budget amounts in the budgeting spreadsheet.

Changing the Screen Layout

The budgeting spreadsheet is displayed in 12 monthly columns. You can change the layout of the screen to display budget amounts by quarter or by year. To change the layout of the budgeting spreadsheet, select one of the following from the Layout pull-down menu:

Quarter—displays budget amounts by quarter (four columns).

Year—displays the budget amounts by year (one column).

You can enter budget amounts by quarter or by year. Then if you select the Month option from the Layout pull-down menu, Quicken distributes the budget amounts evenly across the monthly columns.

Copying Budget Amounts from One File to Another

Quicken allows you to set up your budget amounts in one file and copy them to another file. To copy budget amounts from one file to another, follow these steps:

1. Select the Quicken file with the budget amounts that you want to copy to another file. (See Lesson 22 to learn how to select Quicken files.)

2. Select Set Up Budgets from the Activities pull-down menu in the Write Checks screen or any noninvestment register.

3. Select the Export Budget option from the File pull-down menu. Quicken displays the Save budget to file window.

4. Type a name for the export file in the DOS File field and press Enter to create the file.

5. Select the Quicken file to which you want to copy budget amounts.

6. Access the budgeting spreadsheet.

7. Select the Import Budget option from the File pull-down menu.

8. Type the name of the file that you created in step 4 and press Enter to copy the budget amounts in the budgeting spreadsheet.

Creating Budget Reports

You can create Budget Reports that compare actual amounts with budgeted amounts and show the difference. Quicken provides two different Budget Reports: the Personal Monthly Budget Report and the Custom Budget Report. To create the Personal Monthly Budget Report, refer to Lesson 17. To create the Custom Budget Report, select the Budget report option from the Reports menu.

In the next lesson, you will learn how to create and display graphs.

Lesson 20
Creating
Graphs

In this lesson, you will learn how to create and display graphs using your Quicken data.

With Quicken 6, you can create on-screen graphs to show relationships between your income and expenses, assets and liabilities, actual and budget amounts, and individual investments and total portfolio. If you have an installed graphics card, you can create any one of 21 different graphs. Graphs can be created in just seconds based on the transactions that you enter and categorize, the account balances, budgeted data, and investment transactions entered.

Graphs A *graph* is an on-screen representation of your finances. Graphs show you, for example, the relationship of individual expense categories to your total expenditures. With a graph, you can quickly see what percentage each individual expense category is to your total expenses. Graphs are a visual means for analysis that sometimes have more effect than a list of categories or accounts in a report.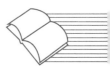

Understanding Graph Formats

Quicken displays graphs in four formats: double-bar, line, pie chart, and stacked bar. You choose which type of graph to create.

- **Double-Bar Graph**—Compares data. The items which the graph compares appear as "bars" and are shown on the horizontal axis, side by side. The dollar amounts or values of the items being compared are shown on the vertical axis.

- **Line Graph**—Shows net values (as a line) over time.

- **Pie Chart**—Shows the composition of each individual item to the whole.

- **Stacked Bar Graph**—Shows trends (like the line graph), however the stacked bar graphs show two trends simultaneously. First it shows the composition of items in the stacked bar, like the composition of total expenses. In this case, each income item is represented by a different color or pattern within each bar. The second trend shows how items are comprised in comparison to the whole, over time.

Setting Up Quicken to Display Graphs

Before you can create and display graphs with Quicken, you must tell Quicken the graphics driver that you are using. To set up Quicken to display graphs, follow these steps:

1. Select Set Preferences from the Main menu.

2. Select Screen Settings and then choose Screen Graphics.

3. Press T to make the text larger or G to make the graph area larger.

4. Press Y to display graphs in black and white (for color monitors).

5. Press F8 to display the list graphics drivers. Use the Up and Down arrows to highlight the graphics driver installed in your system and press Enter.

6. Press Ctrl-Enter.

Creating Graphs

To create a graph, follow these steps:

1. Select View Graphs from the Main menu to display the View Graphs menu shown in Figure 20.1.

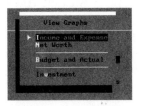

Figure 20.1 The View Graphs menu.

2. From the View Graphs menu, select from the Income and Expense Graphs menu, the Net Worth Graphs menu, the Budget and Actual Graphs menu, or the Investment Graphs menu (see Figure 20.1).

3. Quicken displays the selected menu. Each Graphs menu includes options from which you can choose to create a specific graph. For example, from the Income and Expense Graphs menu, there are six graph options: Monthly Income and Expense, Monthly Income less Expense, Income Composition, Income Trend, Expense Composition, and Expense Trend.

4. Highlight a graph option and press Enter.

5. Quicken displays the graph window like the one shown in Figure 20.2.

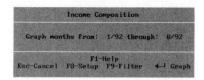

Figure 20.2   The graph window to create an Income Composition graph.

6. Enter the dates that you want to limit transactions to. (Note: Other graph types that you select present other graph settings, such as whether to include unrealized gains, the date to use to graph balances as of, whether to show only income categories, only expense categories or both, or whether to display balances by security, account, type or goal.)

7. Press Ctrl-Enter or F10 to display the graph. Figure 20.3 shows a sample graph.

8. Press Esc to remove the graph from your screen.

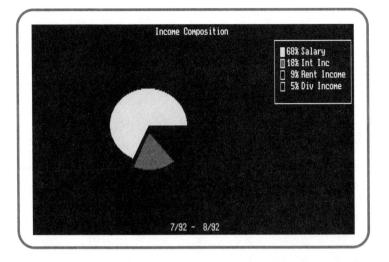

Figure 20.3 An Income Composition graph.

Filtering Transactions in Graphs   If you want to filter graph transactions, press F9-Filter from the graph window. Filtering transactions allows you to restrict the transactions included in the graph, include certain categories and classes, include the current account, all accounts, or select accounts, and so forth.

In the next lesson, you learn how to use Quicken 6's new financial calculators.

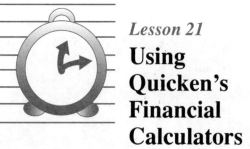

Lesson 21

Using Quicken's Financial Calculators

In this lesson, you learn how to use the financial planning calculators to plan your financial needs for the future.

Financial planning is the process of setting future goals and developing plans to meet those goals. The two primary categories that most people plan for are college (for their children) and retirement. Quicken's Retirement and College Calculators can be used to determine how much money you need to save now, for later. If you're an investor, you want to plan your investments to maximize earnings. The Investment Calculator can help you calculate how much your present investments will be worth in the future. And, with the rise and fall in interest rates, refinancing mortgages has become popular. Quicken's Refinance Calculator shows you whether it's beneficial to refinance your current mortgage.

Accessing Financial Planning Calculators

Quicken 6 includes five financial planning calculators:

- Loan Calculator (see Lesson 16)

- Investment Planning Calculator

- Retirement Planning Calculator

- College Planning Calculator

- Refinance Calculator

To access a financial calculator, follow these steps:

1. From the Write Checks screen or any register, select Financial Planning from the Activities pull-down menu.

2. Quicken displays the Financial Planning menu.

3. Use the Up and Down arrow keys to highlight the calculator that you want to use and press Enter.

4. Quicken displays the calculator on-screen.

5. Press Esc to remove the calculator from the screen.

Changing Calculations You can change the calculation that Quicken performs in each financial planning calculator. To change the calculation, press F8 from the calculator screen. Quicken marks the field that it is currently calculating with a check mark. You cannot make an entry in the field which is designated with the check mark.

Using the Investment Planning Calculator

The Investment Planning Calculator calculates the expected growth of an investment, how much money you need now to have a certain amount in the future, or how

much money you need to contribute periodically to an
investment to have a certain amount in the future.

To use the Investment Planning Calculator, follow
these steps:

1. Access the Investment Planning Calculator (shown in
   Figure 21.1) as explained earlier in this lesson.

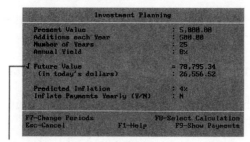

Indicates an amount Quicken has calculated

Figure 21.1   The Investment Planning Calculator.

2. Press F8, if necessary, to move the calculation check
   mark to the field that you want to calculate. You can
   calculate the present value of an investment, the additions each year, or the future value of an investment.

3. Enter the current value of your investment or your
   savings account in the Present Value field. Press Enter.

4. Enter the amount of additional investments or savings
   that you plan to make each year. Press Enter.

5. Enter the number of years you plan to make contributions to your investment account or savings account.
   Press Enter.

Changing Time Periods If you need to change the time period that the Investment Planning Calculator uses in its calculations, press F7 until the time period that you desire is displayed (week, month, quarter, or year). Make sure that you enter the amount of additional investments or savings (in step 4) based on the new time period.

6. Enter the rate of return that you expect from this investment (do not type a percent sign) and press Enter.

7. Enter the current or expected inflation rate and press Enter. Do not type a percent sign.

8. Press Y if you want Quicken to adjust the additions made to your investment or savings account based on the inflation rate, otherwise, press N.

9. Quicken performs the calculation and enters the result in the field marked with the check mark.

Using the Retirement Planning Calculator

The Retirement Planning Calculator calculates how much your retirement account will yield in after-tax annual income at retirement age given your estimated tax rate, yearly contributions, predicted inflation rate, and the expected annual yield. You can also determine how much you need to have now or how much you need to contribute to your retirement account on a yearly basis. To use the Retirement Planning Calculator, follow these steps:

1. Access the Retirement Planning Calculator (shown in Figure 21.2) as explained earlier in this lesson.

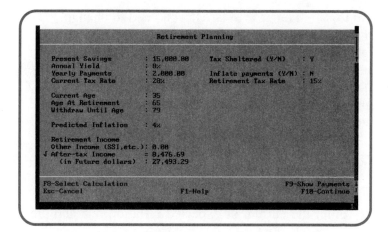

Figure 21.2 The Retirement Planning Calculator.

2. Press F8, if necessary, to move the calculation check mark to the field that you want to calculate. You can calculate the amount of present savings needed, the yearly payments, or the amount of after-tax income at retirement.

3. Enter the amount of your current retirement or savings account in the Present Savings field and press Enter.

4. If your current retirement account is tax-sheltered (not subject to federal income taxes due to a tax law provision), type Y in the Tax Sheltered field.

5. Enter the rate of return that you expect from your retirement or savings account. Don't enter percentages as decimals.

6. Enter the amount that you plan to contribute to your retirement or savings account on a yearly basis. Press Enter.

7. Press Y if you want Quicken to increase your yearly contributions for inflation, or press N to keep your contributions constant. Press Enter.

8. Type your current maximum tax rate without the percent sign. Press Enter.

9. Type your estimated tax rate when you retire and press Enter.

10. In the Current Age field, type your age and press Enter.

11. Type the age at which you're eligible to or would like to retire. Press Enter.

12. In the Withdraw Until Age field, type the age that you hope to live to and press Enter.

13. Type the current inflation rate without the percent sign. Press Enter.

Inflation Rate   The *inflation rate* is the annual percentage rate that prices increase. The $2,000 that you contribute to your retirement account this year, for example, will not be the same as contributing $2,000 ten years from now.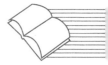

14. In the Other Income field, enter your annual retirement income from social security, pensions, and so forth, and press Enter.

15. Quicken calculates the field designated with the check mark and enters the result.

Using the College Planning Calculator

The College Planning Calculator calculates how much money you need to have today, how much you need to save each year, how much you'll need to send your kids to college in the future, or how to determine how much annual tuition you can afford.

To use the College Planning Calculator, follow these steps:

1. Access the College Planning Calculator (shown in Figure 21.3) as explained earlier in this lesson.

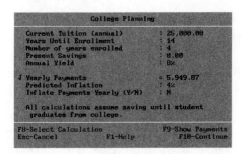

Figure 21.3 The College Planning Calculator.

2. Press F8, if necessary, to move the calculation check mark to the field that you want to calculate: Current Tuition, Present Savings, or Yearly Payments.

3. Enter the current annual tuition for the school that your child plans to attend. Press Enter.

4. Type the number of years between now and the time your child reaches college age and press Enter.

5. Type the number of years that you will be funding your child's education (normally 4). Press Enter.

6. Enter the annual rate of return that you expect to receive on your investment or college savings and press Enter. Do not enter the percent sign.

7. Type the amount, if any, that you will invest or save each year. Press Enter.

8. Enter the expected inflation rate from now until your child begins college. Press Enter.

9. In the Inflate Payments Yearly field, press Y if you want to inflate the yearly payment or press N if you want the payments to remain constant.

10. Quicken performs the calculation and enters the result in the field marked with the check mark.

Using the Refinance Calculator

The Refinance Calculator helps you determine the benefits of refinancing your existing mortgage.

To use the Refinance Calculator, follow these steps:

1. Access the Refinance Calculator (shown in Figure 21.4) as explained earlier in this lesson.

2. In the Existing Mortgage section of the Refinance Calculator, enter your current payment amount in the Current payment field (press Enter) and the escrow amount for insurance, property taxes, and so forth in the Impound/escrow amount field. Press Enter.

3. In the Proposed Mortgage section of the Refinance Calculator, enter the amount that you plan to refinance and press Enter. Remember that this amount is not the

same amount as your original mortgage because you've paid down some principal since the time the mortgage originated.

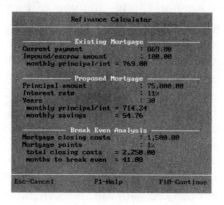

Figure 21.4 The Refinance Calculator.

In the Interest rate field, enter the refinancing rate and press Enter. Don't enter a percent sign. Quicken calculates the new monthly principal and interest payment and your monthly savings (your old monthly principal and interest payment minus the new monthly principal and interest payment).

4. In the last section of the Refinance Calculator (Break Even Analysis) enter any cost you will incur by refinancing, such as closing costs and mortgage points.

5. Quicken calculates the total closing costs to refinance and determines how many months it will take you to break even (how many months it will take you to recover the closing costs using the monthly savings from refinancing).

In the next lesson, you learn how to manage your Quicken files.

Working with Quicken Files

In this lesson, you will learn how to set up new Quicken files, to back up, restore, and copy files, and how to archive files and start a new year.

Quicken works with one file at a time. A *file* is made up of accounts (as many as 255), all of which use the same categories, subcategories, classes, memorized transactions and reports, transaction groups, securities, security types, security goals, security prices, and electronic payees. Reports for Quicken files consolidate data from all or selected accounts within the file. When you start Quicken the first time and set up your first account, Quicken automatically creates a file for you. (Note: In versions of Quicken prior to version 5, files were referred to as account groups).

Setting Up a New Quicken File

You may need to set up a new Quicken file to keep track of transactions that are unrelated to your present file. To set up a new file, follow these steps:

1. Select Set Preferences from the Main menu and then select File Activities.

2. From the next window, choose the Select/Set Up File option to display the Select/Set Up New File window shown in Figure 22.1.

149

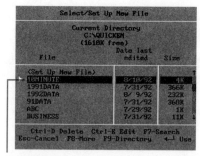

Selecting a file to use

Figure 22.1 The Select/Set Up New File window.

3. Position the arrow on the <Set Up New File> line and press Enter.

4. Quicken displays the Set Up New File window shown in Figure 22.2.

5. Type a name for the new file (up to 8 characters; do not include symbols such as . /\[ ] : < > + = ; , ' "). Press Enter.

6. Type the drive and directory where you want the data files created. Quicken automatically enters the default directory—C:\QUICKEN. Press Enter.

7. At the Standard Categories window, type the number that corresponds to the categories you want to use.

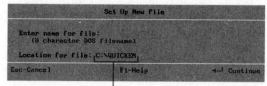

The drive and directory where the new file is to be located

Figure 22.2 The Set Up New File window for defining a new Quicken file.

8. Press Enter to add the new file to the Select/Set Up New File list.

Editing and Deleting Quicken Files   You can edit or delete a file from the Select/Set Up New File window. To edit a file, position the arrow on the file and press Ctrl-E to select the Edit option. To delete a file, press Ctrl-D to select the Delete option.

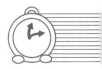

Searching for Quicken Files   To do a quick search for Quicken data files in any location, press F7 from the Select/Set Up New File window. Then type the letter of the drive that you want to search and press Enter. Quicken displays all of the data files that it found. Position the arrow on any file you want to use or press F8 to see additional information, such as the date you last edited the file, file size, and so forth.

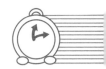

Selecting a File to Use

If you have more than one file, you must select the file that you want to use each time you start Quicken. To select a file to use, follow these steps:

1. Select Set Preferences from the Main menu and then select the File Activities option.

2. From the next window, choose the Select/Set Up File option to display the Select/Set Up New File window.

3. Position the arrow on the file that you want to use and press Enter. (Press F9 if you need to change the directory to look for a file.)

Changing the Drive and the Directory

You can change the directory where Quicken looks for your data files. To change the directory, follow these steps:

1. Select Set Preferences from the Main menu and then select the File Activities option.

2. From the next window, select the Set File Location option to display the Set File Location window.

3. Type the drive and directory where your Quicken data files are located and press Enter.

Backing Up Files

To protect yourself from losing important data, you should make a backup copy of each of your Quicken files on a regular basis. To back up a *selected* file, follow these steps:

1. Select Set Preferences from the Main menu and then select the File Activities option.

2. At the next window, select the Back Up File option.

3. Quicken displays the Select Backup Drive window. Type the drive letter for the backup disk and press Enter.

4. From the File list, displayed next, use the Up and Down arrow keys to position the arrow on the file that you want to back up.

5. Press Enter to begin the backup process.

To back up the *current* file, follow these steps:

1. From the Write Checks screen or any register, select Back up File from the Print/Acct pull-down menu.

2. Type the drive letter for the backup disk.

3. Press Enter to begin the backup process.

Quick Backups   You can make a quick backup of the current file from the Main menu. Just press Ctrl-B to access the Back up option or Ctrl-E to access the Back up and Exit option.

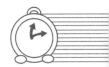

Restoring a File

You may need to restore a file if something happens to your hard disk. To restore a file, follow these steps:

1. Select Set Preferences from the Main menu and then select the File Activities option.

2. At the next window, select the Restore File option.

3. Quicken instructs you to insert your Backup Disk in a drive. After your disk is inserted, type the drive letter and press Enter.

4. From the File list, position the arrow on the file that you want to restore.

5. Press Enter to restore data to the file.

Copying Files

You may want to copy all or part of a Quicken file to start a new file. To copy a file:

1. Select the file that you want to copy from.

2. Select Set Preferences from the Main menu and then select the File Activities option.

3. At the next window, select the Copy File option to display the Copy File window.

4. Type the DOS file name for the new file and press Enter.

5. Type the path (drive and/or directory) where the new file will be located. Press Enter.

6. Type the beginning and ending dates for transactions to be copied and press Enter.

7. Press Y if you want to copy prior uncleared transactions, or N if you do not. Press Enter.

8. If you have investment accounts set up in the file that you are copying, press Y to copy all investment transactions, or N if you do not want investment transactions copied.

9. Press F9 if you want to set the maximum number of accounts that can be created in the new file (up to 255). Quicken automatically sets the maximum amount to 64.

10. Press Ctrl-Enter to start copying.

11. When the copy procedure is complete, Quicken lets you continue using your original file or start using the new file.

Closing Quicken Files

At the end of the year or your accounting period, you may want to close your Quicken file before entering transactions for the new year. Quicken provides you with two options for closing files: the Archive option and the Start New Year option.

Archiving Data

The Archive option copies all transactions from prior years to an archive file. For example, let's say that the current date is January 1, 1993; when you select the Archive option, all transactions dated December 31, 1992 and earlier are copied to an archive file. The current file remains untouched. To archive data from prior years, follow these steps:

1. Select Set Preferences from the Main menu and then select the File Activities option.

2. At the next window, select the Year End option to display the Year End window shown in Figure 22.3.

3. Press 1 to select the Archive option.

4. Quicken displays the Archive File window. Quicken enters the file name, archive file location, and the archive transaction dates. Make any necessary changes to the Archive File window.

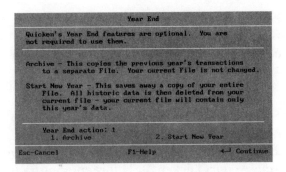

Figure 22.3 The Year End window to archive Quicken data.

5. Press Ctrl-Enter to create the archive file.

Starting a New Year

The Start New Year option creates an archive file for all transactions from prior years and then deletes prior year transactions from the current file. (Note: Quicken never deletes uncleared transactions or investment transactions. After you perform the Start New Year procedure, your current file will contain only those transactions from the current year.)

To start a new year, follow these steps:

1. Select Set Preferences from the Main menu and then select the File Activities option.

2. At the next window, select the Year End option to display the Year End window.

3. Press 2 to select the Start New Year option.

4. Quicken displays the Start New Year window. Type a name for the archive file that Quicken will create and press Enter.

5. Type the date of the first transaction you want to remain in your current file.

6. Press Ctrl-Enter to create a file for the new year and delete transactions from previous years.

7. Specify which file you want to use: the old file or the file for the new year.

This lesson concludes your course through the *10 Minute Guide to Quicken 6.*

Index